500 WORLD WAR I & II FACTS

SCOTT MATTHEWS

Copyright © 2016 Scott Matthews

All rights reserved. No part of this publication may be reproduced, distributed or transmitted in any form or by any means, including photocopying, recording, or other electronic or mechanical methods, without the prior written permission of the publisher, except in the case of brief quotations embodied in critical reviews and certain other non-commercial uses permitted by copyright law.

Trademarked names appear throughout this book. Rather than use a trademark symbol with every occurrence of a trademarked name, names are used in an editorial fashion, with no intention of infringement of the respective owner's trademark. The information in this book is distributed on an "as is" basis, without warranty. Although every precaution has been taken in the preparation of this work, neither the author nor the publisher shall have any liability to any person or entity with respect to any loss or damage caused or alleged to be caused directly or indirectly by the information contained in this book.

ABOUT THE AUTHOR

Scott Matthews is a geologist, world traveller and author of the 'Amazing World Facts' series! He was born in Brooklyn New York by immigrant parents from Ukraine but grew up in North Carolina. Scott studied at Duke University where he graduated with a degree in Geology and History. His studies allowed him to travel the globe where he saw and learned amazing trivial knowledge with his many encounters. With the vast amount of interesting information he accumulated he created his best selling books "Random, Interesting and Fun Facts You Need To Know".

He hopes this book will provide you with hours of fun, knowledge, entertainment and laughter.

If you gain any knowledge from this book, think it's fun and could put a smile on someone's face, he would greatly appreciate your review on Amazon.

BONUS

Thanks for supporting me and purchasing this book! I'd like to send you some freebies. They include:

- The digital version of *500 World War I & II Facts*

- The digital version of *101 Idioms and Phrases*

- The audiobook for my best seller *1144 Random Facts*

Go to the last page of the book and scan the QR code. Enter your email and I'll send you all the files. Happy reading!

7 BENEFITS OF READING FACTS

1. Knowledge
2. Stress Reduction
3. Mental Stimulation
4. Better Writing Skills
5. Vocabulary Expansion
6. Memory Improvement
7. Stronger Analytical Thinking Skills

In the midst of chaos, there is also opportunity.

— SUN TZU

PART I
WORLD WAR I

WWI Timeline

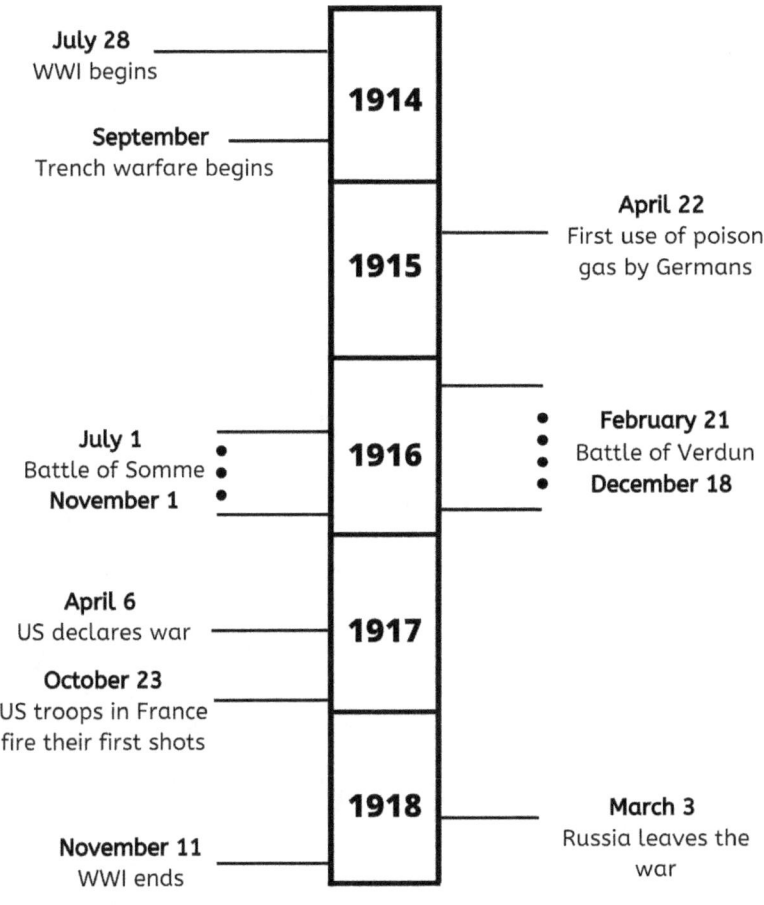

250 FACTS

1) Right before the war, Europe was divided into two main alliances. The Triple Entente included Britain, Russia, and France. The Triple Alliance included Germany, Italy, and Austro-Hungary.

2) Italy went back on its word to the Triple Alliance when the war started, and it failed to join the war when it broke out in 1914.

3) In the decade leading up to WWI, Germany and Britain had a naval arms race. Britain won the race because it was able to acquire thirty-eight battleships while Germany only had twenty-four.

4) Before the war started in 1914, France and Russia had 928,000 more soldiers than Austro-Hungary and Germany. This means the Triple Entente had a numerical advantage over the Triple Alliance. Great Britain had a standing army of 248,000 which was very small compared to other major countries at the time.

5) The Balkan States (a collection of countries in Eastern Europe that included Greece, Serbia, Bulgaria, Macedonia, and Bosnia), were engaged in two consecutive wars in 1912 and 1913, and in the end, Serbia emerged as a nationalist state.

6) At the beginning of the war, Russia mobilized 5 million men, Germany mobilized 4.5 million men, France mobilized 3.8 million men, and Britain mobilized 0.75 million men.

7) Britain wanted to recruit 200,000 men in the first month of the war, but they surpassed their target when 300,000 men enlisted. Throughout the duration of the war, about 2.5 million Britons volunteered for the war, but only a quarter of them were eligible for enlistment.

British soldiers walking to Somme

8) When the war started in 1914, many in Britain thought that it would be over very soon, and those who joined the army expected that they would be home by Christmas.

9) Compulsory enlistment into the army was introduced in Britain in 1916. Roughly 750,000 British citizens appealed against compulsory enlistment in the first six months after it came into effect. Most of them were given temporary exemptions so that they could get their affairs in order before joining the army. Those who refused to fight out of principle, and for no other reason, were each given a white feather as a symbol of their cowardice.

10) In 1914, the British Empire had more than 400 million people, and Britain could bring in fighters from India and other territories.

11) 27% of all Scotsmen between the ages of fifteen and forty nine volunteered for the war before the end of 1915.

12) In 1917, The Russian Government started "Battalions of Death" that consisted entirely of female soldiers. These battalions were never put on the battlefront, but they were used to shame Russian male soldiers into fighting harder.

13) For the entire war, Germany mobilized 13.4 million men in total. This was the highest number of any country that took part in WWI.

14) The longest battle in the entire war was called the Battle of Verdun. It started in February 1916 and ended in December 1916, lasting more than 300 days. The bloodiest battle in the entire war was called The Battle of Somme. On the first day alone, Britain lost 60,000 troops. In total, Britain lost 460,000 men, France lost 200,000 men, and Germany lost 500,000 men.

15) When the war started in 1914, none of the armies offered their soldiers equipment or uniforms that were designed to meet the demands of modern warfare. They all had colorful uniforms and soft hats, which made them easy targets in the battlefield. All countries adopted the use of steel helmets and camouflage outfits during the course of the war.

16) The use of trenches in WWI started in September 1914. Digging trenches was necessary because both sides had sophisticated machine guns that could fire 600 rounds per minute and mow down soldiers in open fields.

Trench warfare

17) Germany pioneered the use of flamethrowers in battle in February, 1915. Their flamethrowers could shoot jets of fire up to 130 feet (40 meters) long.

18) Military tanks were first used in battle on September 15, 1916, during what came to be called The Battle of Somme. Tanks were supposed to be called "land-ships,"

but Britain named them "tanks" in order to make German spies think that they were building water tanks and not weapons.

19) Soldiers would often build mine shafts through no man's land in order to place and blow up explosives beneath enemy lines before major assaults. Some explosives used in the war were so loud they could be heard miles away. In 1917, explosives going off underneath German lines at Messines Ridge (Ypres) were heard 139 miles (225 kilometres) away in London.

20) Both sides used toxic gas during the war. 1.2 million soldiers were killed in gas attacks while many more were injured and disfigured.

Soldiers wearing gas masks

21) More than seventy different types of aircraft were used in WWI. At first, they were mostly used for spying on the enemy, but as the war progressed, they were increasingly used as fighters and bombers.

22) British whippet tanks were instrumental in the allies' success near the end of the war because they were faster and more flexible than German machines.

23) The aviator term "dogfight" actually originated in WWI. Pilots had to switch off engines mid-air to keep the planes from stalling during sharp turns. The pilots noticed that when they restarted the engines, they sounded like barking dogs. As a result, mid-air confrontations with enemy pilots were named dog-fights.

24) Over twelve million letters were sent from Britain to France every week. Even during the war it only took two days for a letter to be delivered.

25) On May 7th, 1915, a German submarine attacked a civilian cruise line, killing roughly 1,200 people, 128 of whom were Americans. This influenced America's decision to join WWI on the side of the allies.

26) During WWI, German submarine (U-boat) attacks were so common in the Atlantic Ocean that 1.4 million tonnes of supplies shipped by the allies were sunk in a span of three months in late 1916. Germany constructed 360 submarine U-boats. Of those, 176 were destroyed during the war. German U-boat submarines managed to sink half of all British merchant ships in an effort to weaken the British economy during the war.

27) The greatest sea battle of WWI was called the Battle of Jutland. It took place from May 31st to June 1st, 1916. The fighting was so intense that the British navy lost fourteen battleships, while the German navy lost eleven battleships.

28) During WWI, it was almost impossible to navigate the North Sea because both sides of the conflict used heavy mines there. This was done in violation of a standing 1907 treaty that restricted the use of mines near an enemy's coastline.

29) The allies imposed a naval blockade of Germany from August 1914 to January 1919. This plan was very effective because Germany relied heavily on imports. Scholars estimate that 424,000 German lives were lost as a result of the blockade.

30) In Britain, more than 700,000 women were employed in factories that manufactured weapons during the war.

31) In Britain, there were about 16,000 soldiers who refused to fight for moral reasons. A few of them were put in non-combatant roles in the army, while the rest were sent to prison.

32) In all European countries, women and civilians who stayed home during the war died at very high rates because of malnutrition. Germany, in particular, experienced hundreds of thousands of deaths due to a combination of starvation and hunger-related illnesses.

33) Before WWI, it was rare for women to work in factories, but by the end of the war, between 36% - 37% of the industrial workforce in both France and Britain was female.

Women in munitions production factory

34) In Germany, turnips were considered animal feed until the winter of 1916, when they were used to feed people because of potato and meat shortages. That winter is still known as "Turnip Winter" in Germany. Similarly, meat became very scarce in Germany during the war. By the end of 1916, the meat supply had dropped to 31% compared to peacetime supply, and by the end of 1918, it had gone as low as 12%.

35) An Australian war hero named Private Billy Sing is credited with killing over 150 Turkish soldiers when he was a sniper during WWI. He earned the nickname "murderer" from his fellow soldiers.

36) A German pilot named Ernst Udet flew sixty one successful missions during WWI, making him one of the best pilots at the time.

37) A lone Portuguese soldier named Anibal Milhais was able to single-handedly withstand two German assaults. During the ongoing gunfight, he fought so hard that he

convinced the German soldiers that they were dealing with an entire army unit, instead of just one soldier.

38) A British nurse named Edith Cavell helped 200 allied soldiers escape from Belgium, which was occupied by Germany at the time.

39) A sixteen-year-old boy named John Cornwell was the youngest soldier to be awarded the Victoria Cross (the highest and most prestigious award of the British honours system). Despite getting a fatal wound, he held his post for over an hour.

40) Dogs had many crucial roles in the war, and they were used by both sides. Their roles included carrying supplies, locating wounded soldiers, sniffing out enemy positions, delivering messages across the battlefield, and companionship. About one million dogs lost their lives on the battlefield during WWI.

41) Homing pigeons were very important messengers during the war. In Britain, they even passed a law that would punish the killing, wounding or molesting of homing pigeons with up to six months of jail time. A homing pigeon named Cher Ami is credited with saving the lives of 194 American soldiers who were trapped behind enemy lines. Cher managed to reach her loft and deliver her message despite being shot through the chest and losing her vision in one eye.

42) A total of approximately eight million horses were killed in the war.

43) There were approximately 37.5 million casualties whose deaths were directly related to the WWI conflict. Seven million soldiers were permanently injured or crippled for the rest of their lives after the war. It's estimated that 230 soldiers died every hour during WWI.

44) Shell shock was a common condition that affected soldiers on both sides of the war. 80,000 British servicemen suffered from shell shock as a result of the war. It was a mental condition that resulted from spending a lot of time on battlefields with intense artillery shelling.

45) The central powers spent $11,345 for every soldier they killed during WWI. The allies spent $36,486 for every soldier they killed.

46) To encourage support for the war back at home, Britain made and distributed war-themed toys, including toy tanks and toy soldiers.

47) An elephant named Lizzie was enlisted in the British army, and she was used to transport munitions into battle.

48) A Boston terrier bulldog named Stubby was trained to detect incoming shells before the soldiers could hear them. He would start barking, and soldiers would know that it was time to take cover. He was so good at his job that he officially earned the title Sergeant Stubby.

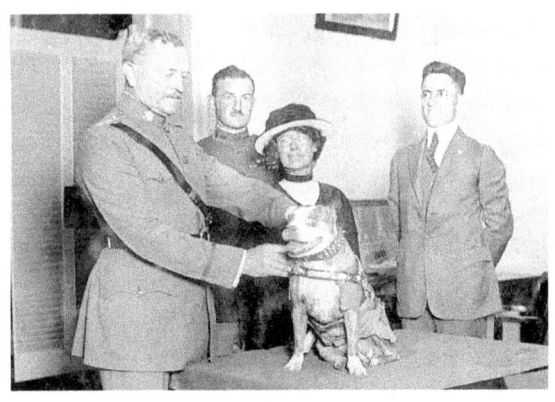
John Pershing awards Sergeant Stubby with a medal

49) Sometimes, cats were brought along to serve as mascots for various army units. One such example was Peter the cat, who accompanied a unit called the Northumberland Hussars.

50) Two out of every three Australian soldiers who went to fight in WWI didn't make it back home alive.

51) When WWI ended, 11% of all French people were either dead or wounded.

52) As a result of WWI, four whole empires collapsed. They included the Austro-Hungarian Empire, The Ottoman Empire, the Russian Empire, and the German Empire. Several modern countries including Estonia, Lithuania, Finland, Latvia, and Poland, rose as independent nations from the ashes of WWI.

53) When the war ended, Germany was forced to take responsibility for the whole war, and to pay $31.4 billion to the allies as compensation for damages and loss of life.

Adjusted for inflation, that's equivalent to $442 billion in today's cash.

54) Thirty different countries were directly involved in WWI.

55) When the British army started building tanks, they categorized them into female and male tanks. The female ones were fitted with machine guns, while the male ones were fitted with cannons.

56) The German army used terror tactics to keep civilians in occupied territories from rebelling. At one point, they shot 150 civilians in Belgium to show the rest that their orders were to be obeyed.

57) America refused to take sides at the start of WWI. Some American citizens who wanted to help the allies, took their own initiative and joined the French, Canadian, and British Armies.

58) US President Woodrow Wilson was re-elected in 1916 on a promise to keep America out of WWI. However, just one month after he was sworn in, he felt obligated to declare war on Germany.

59) America drafted 2.7 million men to join the US Army during WWI with an additional 1.3 million men volunteering later to join.

60) The Spanish Flu accounted for one third of all military deaths during WWI. It was very easy for soldiers to become sick because the trenches were extremely dirty and full of bacteria.

61) Even though the US was late in joining the allied war effort, it spent $30 billion during WWI.

62) Nine out of ten British soldiers survived when they were in the trenches. British soldiers rarely saw the firing lines during the war and were always moving around the trenches. This allowed them to keep away from the dangers of enemy fire.

63) Based on casualty figures, WWI is the sixth deadliest conflict in human history.

64) At the time, WWI was referred to by many different names, including "The World War," "The Great War," "The War to End All Wars," and "The War of the Nations."

65) Soldiers whose faces were disfigured during WWI often wore special masks to cover their wounds or scars. These masks only covered the disfigured parts of the face, and they were painted to look like the rest of the face.

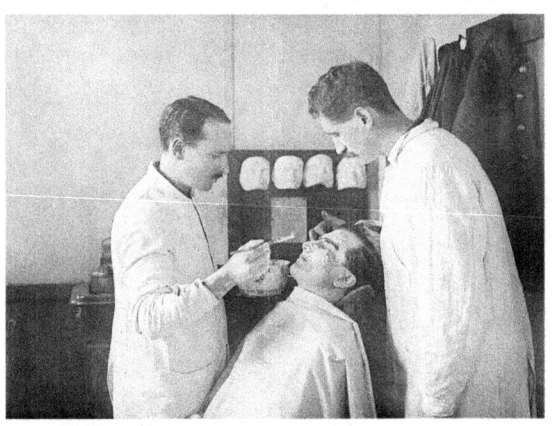

Soldier with facial injuries has a plaster cast made

66) Although most of the fighting occurred on European soil, the WWI conflicts spilled over to all oceans and all habitable continents in the world.

67) Three-quarters of all Russian soldiers who fought in the war were either killed, wounded or unaccounted for by the time Russia left the war.

68) German trenches were better constructed than British trenches. They were equipped with electricity, water taps, bunk beds, furniture, and some rooms even had doorbells.

69) In the case of gas attacks, soldiers on both sides of the conflict were trained to soak pieces of cloth in urine and hold them over their faces. It wasn't until 1918 that proper gas masks were provided to the soldiers.

70) During the war, the French developed a cannon that could shoot accurately up to 4 miles (about 6.4kms). The Germans feared it so much that they called it the "Devil Gun." French commanders believed that the allies won the war because of this one weapon.

71) When the US joined WWI, most moviegoers in America had to sit through four-minute pro-war speeches before they could watch any films.

72) American foods of German origin were renamed during WWI because people started to dislike German culture. Hamburgers became Salisbury steaks, dachshunds became liberty dogs, and frankfurters became liberty sausages.

73) 200,000 African Americans were enlisted in the Army during WWI. The army had segregated divisions so they

were trained separately. Only 11% of them were put in combat roles, while most of them were given manual labor roles. 13,000 Native Americans served in the US Military in WWI, although they were not granted US Citizenship until a few years after the war had ended.

74) Germans were very good at intercepting and breaking the codes used by the allies in the early stages of WWI. This continued until the United States decided to use lesser-known Native American languages for their coded messages. Members of the Choctaw tribe were put in charge of encoding messages, and from that point on, Germans couldn't translate any of the messages.

75) The United States became the world's greatest military power during WWI. The country underwent a broad military build-up as they prepared to join the war.

76) The Turks killed approximately 1.5 million Armenian civilians during WWI. This genocide went mostly unnoticed at the time because other countries were so busy fighting the war that they couldn't intervene or raise concerns.

77) WWI helped to fast-track the liberation of women. When men were off fighting the war, women took over many jobs that were reserved for men. By the time the war ended, it was clear to everyone that women were just as capable as men in the workplace. Older women in Britain were even given the right to vote before the war ended. The US granted women the right to vote in 1920, the year of the first major election after the war.

78) After WWI, Britain lost its leadership position in the world economy because it had spent so much money and resources, lost so many people, and incurred heavy damages during the war.

79) The WWI trenches covered over 25,000 miles (40,000 kms). They started on the English Channel and extended all the way to Switzerland.

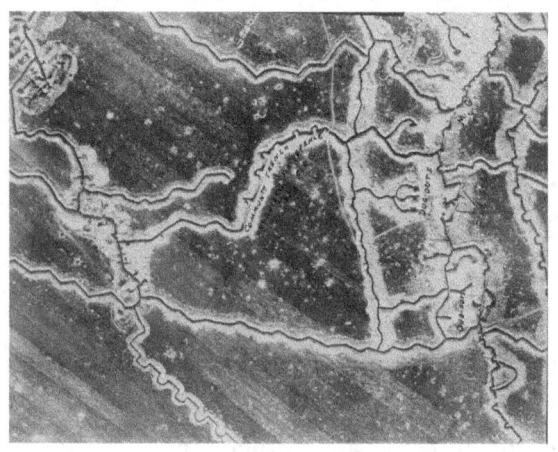

Aerial photograph of WW1 trenches

80) When the war started, Britain cut all German undersea cables. That way, the allies were the only ones who were able to send quick messages to the United States.

81) Britain had a secret publication task force called The Wellington House during the war. It published war picture books in different languages and distributed them in major countries across the world. Those books helped to turn several countries (e.g. China) against Germany.

82) In 1917, President Woodrow Wilson created a Committee on Public information which used many different tactics, including creating pro-war films, posters, pamphlets, adverts, and books to convince Americans to support the war. The committee also paid clergymen and professors to give pro-war sermons and lectures to people in churches and colleges.

83) Right after the war started, Germany was working on plans to turn Central and Western Europe into a common market that they would control to their benefit. This means that if Germany had won WWI, most of Europe would be economically dependent on the country.

84) To raise money for the war, allied governments issued war bonds. This was the first time many people were introduced to financial securities. In America, war bonds were called Liberty Bonds, and buying them was considered a patriotic duty.

"Defend your country with your dollars"

85) Britain joined the war partly because it feared both outcomes of a war where it wasn't involved. If Germany and Austria-Hungary had won, Britain wouldn't have any friends left in Europe. If France and Russia had won, they wouldn't be too happy about Britain not helping out, and they would cut ties with the country. Either way, Britain would have lost respect around the world, especially in places like India and the Mediterranean (where it had many colonies). Therefore, Britain decided that it had no choice but to join.

86) WWI ended at 11 o'clock on 11th November, 1918.

87) There was a minimum height requirement for the British Army which was five foot three. Shorter men were recruited however, and a new role was created for them known as the 'Bantam Battalions'. This consisted of mining and tunnelling where their height was an advantage.

88) When the war started, Germany fought on two fronts. They invaded France (through Belgium) on the Western Front, and they fought Russia in the Eastern Front. Russia was never able to break through any of Germany's defense lines on the Eastern Front.

89) Russia's losses in the war caused serious problems back home. The war caused poverty, food scarcity, and economic instability. As a result, Russians revolted against Czar Nicolas II and ended his regime. They particularly disliked the Czar because his wife was born in Germany. Due to this Revolution, the country stopped participating in WWI in 1917.

90) President Woodrow Wilson went to congress and declared war on Germany on April 2nd, 1917. This happened right after Germany sank four American merchant ships that were transporting supplies to Britain.

91) During WWI, Winston Churchill served in the military as First Lord of British Admiralty. He resigned from his post after a failed military campaign, and he took another post with a French battalion.

92) Italy joined the war on the side of the allied powers on May 23rd, 1915, when it declared war on Austria-Hungary.

93) The British Navy made a surprise attack on docked German vessels in early 1915. They hoped that Germans would be willing to confront them in a naval battle at the time, but Germany knew they had a weaker navy so they avoided conflicts at sea for that entire year.

94) Although planes were widely used in the war, they didn't make as much of an impact as British battleships and German submarines.

95) Britain created the Royal Air force on April 1st, 1918, becoming the first country in the world to have an air force that was independent of other branches of the military.

96) Germany launched its very last WWI offense on 15th July, 1918. This came to be known as the Second Battle of Marne.

97) WWI created the opportunity for Afghanistan to break away from British control and to become an independent

country. Britain's resources were drained after the war, so they readily gave in when Afghanistan pushed for independence.

98) The war heavily contributed to the spread of the Spanish flu that infected one-third of the world's population. Soldiers who returned to their home countries around the world spread the flu, which resulted in many more deaths than the actual war.

99) Unlike the tanks used today, those used in WWI were very crude. They were hard to drive, the inside was noisy, filled with smoke, and they didn't have shock absorbers which made the soldiers inside bounce around all the time. The soldiers who operated the tanks had to wear masks to protect their faces as enemy fire would produce sharp pieces of steel that would fly around inside. In the latter stages of WWI, Renault, the car company, designed a light tank that could be mass-produced. This gave France and the allied powers a great advantage, and contributed to their victory.

The British Mark V-star Tank

100) Britain caught many German spies on its soil during the war. Eleven spies were executed at the Tower of London.

101) Before WWI, wrist watches were rare, and they were mostly worn by high-class women as jewellery. Men often carried pocket watches. Wristwatches became common during WWI because it was hard for men (mostly soldiers) to use pocket watches while fighting in the trenches.

102) Barbed wire was widely used during the war to protect the trenches, and to direct enemy soldiers towards "kill zones."

103) The term "crimes against humanity" was first used in a joint statement by allied forces in May 1915. In that statement, they rebuked the Ottoman Empire for killing more than half of all Armenian civilians, and they accused the Turks of committing crimes against humanity.

104) Trench coats got their name from WWI trenches. Although these kinds of coats existed before the war, they became popular during the war because they were specially designed and issued to British military officers, some of whom supervised the war in the trenches.

105) When the war started, the world was mostly powered by horses, as well as coal and steam engines. The nature of WWI forced the world to adopt the use of oil at a faster pace. Aircraft, submarines, tanks, and new battleships all used internal combustion engines, so the demand for oil increased.

106) A medical condition known as "trench foot" was very common during the war. Soldiers wore tight boots in water-logged trenches for days or even weeks. Their legs would swell and rot, and even had to be cut off sometimes.

107) **WWI** caused one of the worst refugee crises in European history. It's estimated that more than 7.5 million people were displaced during the war.

Jewish refugees from Lublin, Poland, on the road to Austrian lines

108) Blood transfusions became popular during WWI. Although the procedure had been attempted a few times before the war, the modern techniques used to preserve blood, and to differentiate between blood types, were developed just as the war started.

109) Ireland broke away from Britain to become an independent country mostly because of events that played out during WWI. The UK and Ireland were sorting out governance issues in early 1914, but that was put on hold when the war broke out, which was very disappointing to

the Irish people. Ireland also disliked Britain's decision to draft Irishmen into the army. After WWI, Ireland declared independence and won.

110) Tunnel digging was one of the most feared jobs on the Western Front. Diggers were often killed by collapsing tunnel roofs, gas attacks, or explosives.

111) Guided missiles were first invented during WWI, but they were never actually used in the war because they failed to work accurately during tests.

112) Vegetarian sausages were invented during WWI by the mayor of Cologne as an alternative to meat, which was scarce and expensive at the time.

113) Mustard gas was first used as a chemical weapon in 1917. Unlike other gases, it was hard to detect, and it was very lethal.

114) WWI was the first war fought after the assembly line was perfected. As a result, industrial mass production changed the way the war was fought. Britain, Germany, and France all used assembly lines to produce munitions, tanks, vehicles, and planes in record high numbers.

115) President Woodrow Wilson came up with a fourteen point plan that would have ensured peace after the war, but he lacked the necessary political support both in America and Europe to execute that plan.

116) Palestine was part of the Ottoman Empire when WWI started. The allies promised the local Arab tribes that they could keep Palestinian land if they helped to fight the Turks. However, when the Ottoman Empire fell,

Britain went back on its word and colonized Palestine. Americans were unhappy with Britain's imperial ambitions, so Britain decided to establish a national home for the Jewish people in Palestine in order to appease the United States. Those events set the stage for the Middle-East conflict that persists to date.

117) Surgeons started wearing blue scrubs during WWI. Soldiers used to die in high numbers after surgery due to infections. A French doctor named Rene Leriche figured out that the infections could be prevented if the clothes used by surgeons were color-coded so that they wouldn't be mixed with other supplies during transportation. The practice was quickly adopted throughout France, and it rapidly spread to other countries.

118) WWI led to the nationalization of railways throughout Europe. Railways were very important during the war because they were used to transport soldiers and bulky supplies to the battlefront, and to move wounded soldiers away from the action. Governments in Europe had to take over all railway operations from smaller companies to ensure that the trains always ran uninterrupted.

En route to the front line

119) To help with the labor shortages during the war, France and Britain recruited 135,000 Chinese nationals and brought them over by sea to Europe. Some of them returned to China after the war, but others stayed and started Chinese communities in cities like Paris.

120) The common medical practice known as 'triage' started during WWI. During the war, doctors often dealt with a high number of injured patients at the same time, so they had to create a system that allowed them to prioritize patient treatment in a way that would increase the number of survivors. Triage is still used today in emergency rooms and during disasters.

121) Political cartoons and caricatures were very popular during WWI. Most pictures from the war were too horrifying to print on newspapers, so cartoons were used instead. Caricatures also came in handy as propaganda tools. For example, in Britain, allied soldiers were drawn as big and strong, while German soldiers were drawn as small, weak, or evil-looking.

Propaganda of Hitler & Tojo

122) The idea of daylight-savings time was proposed a few times before the war started, but it was first introduced in Germany in 1916 as a way to save energy and to make more use of daylight hours. Britain was the second country to introduce it just a few weeks after Germany. The US and France followed suit soon after.

123) When the United States joined WWI, it was so worried about German spies that it introduced the Espionage Act of 1917 and the Sedition Act of 1918. Some people were prosecuted under these Acts, just for speaking up against the war, and many were concerned that it would end Freedom of Speech. Fortunately, those two Acts were revised after the war, and people could criticize the government again without fear.

124) Aircraft carriers were first used in battle during WWI. Before the war, planes could take off from ship decks, but no one had figured out how to land them back

on the ships. For most of the war, Britain, France, Russia, and Germany used sea-planes that would land near the ship before they were dragged on-board using cranes. Towards the end of the war, Britain built two ships on which they could land their smaller fighters.

125) WWI gave way to the rise of communism in Russia. The death and famine that resulted from the war caused the resentment of the ruling class to boil over. The people had a revolution and the Bolshevik Party came into power and became the world's first socialist state in 1917. This led to the creation of the Soviet Union just a few years after the war.

126) Poppies became the remembrance symbol of WWI because of a poem called "In Flanders Fields", which was written by a Canadian surgeon named John McCrae during the war. At the end of the war, an American woman named Moina Michael started offering people imitation poppies to raise money for poor veterans, and her idea quickly spread throughout the world.

127) Metallic prosthetic limbs became popular as a result of WWI. Custom-made wooden prosthetic limbs existed before the war, but only the rich could afford to buy them. As many people lost their limbs during the war, the British government contracted a private company to supply artificial metal limbs to former servicemen.

128) WWI changed the way women dressed. Before the war, women wore hobble skirts (long skirts that narrowed around the ankles) and other clothes that looked luxurious but restricted free movement. But as the war went on,

women had to take up traditional male jobs, so they began wearing clothes that were more practical.

129) WWI cemented the position of the US as a world power. The US was already the biggest economy in the world by 1913. The war devastated European powers so much that even the victors (Britain and France) were left in debt. The US on the other hand, joined the war later, and none of the battles were fought on its soil, affecting them less severely. Their economy had ample time to grow as the war raged on. Russia, Britain, and France relied heavily on the US for financial support during the war, and they took loans from America in order to rebuild after the war.

130) WWI ushered in large-scale industrial production of food. Before the war, most people ate fresh foods, which they grew in their own farms or bought from farmers' markets. However, during the war, European countries had to figure out how to feed hundreds of thousands of soldiers in the trenches. Food processing factories started cropping up all over France, Britain, and many other countries. Canned foods, in particular, were produced in large quantities. After the war, processed foods became staples in all households.

131) WWI helped to forge Canada's identity as a nation in its own right. Canada joined the war as a British Dominion. Although it was still a British Dominion when the war ended, it had become more self-directed (it had its own seat at the League of Nations, and it technically had its own army), although it remained a part of the British Empire for another twelve years.

132) As America recruited soldiers for the war, many factories in northern States were left without workers, and this led to the migration of more than 500,000 African Americans from southern States to northern cities such as New York, Chicago, and Detroit. This led to cultural integration in America, and it set the stage for the civil rights movement.

133) After Germany was defeated, it lost its empire. Its colonies in Africa and Asia were taken away by Britain and France, West Prussia (a part of the former German Empire) was given to Poland, and Alsace-Lorraine (its most economically productive region) was given to France.

134) Grenades were first mass-produced during WWI. They were also modified to be rocket-launched for the first time during the war.

135) One of the worst rail disasters occurred in May of 1915 when a troop train carrying hundreds of men crashed into a stationary train. Minutes later another train crashed into the wreckage of the previous two trains and the whole site caught fire, killing over two hundred people.

136) Cuba's economy grew during WWI because of sugar exports to Europe. Before the war, Europe relied on France's beet crop for sugar production, but since the beet fields had become fighting grounds, sugar production suffered. In the first two years of the war, Cuba built a dozen sugar mills, which were mostly financed by American investors.

137) On Christmas 1914, British and German soldiers who had been fighting for months called an unofficial

cease-fire. They met halfway on no man's land, shook hands, and toasted to each others' good health. During that first year of the war, life was especially hard in the trenches on the Western Front. When Christmas came around, both sides were homesick, and they started singing hymns. Soon, they were taking turns listening to each others hymns. In Ypres (Belgium), foot soldiers at the frontlines called a truce, emerged from the trenches and even supposedly played a friendly soccer match.

138) During the war, a mine explosion killed 10,000 German soldiers. To date, this is still considered to be the deadliest non-nuclear explosion of all time.

139) As a result of WWI, New York overtook London as the leading financial center in the world. Before the war, London was the world's only financial center; it was at the heart of the greatest empire at the time, and the Sterling Pound was very stable and highly credible. But just a few months before the war started, American banks were, for the first time, allowed to open foreign branches outside the US, so they started providing services for major businesses in all continents. By the end of WWI, Britain was in debt, and American banks were financing trade across the world.

140) When WWI started, many heads of European dynasties were related by blood. King George V of Britain, Kaiser Wilhelm II of Germany, and Czar Nicholas II of Russia were all Queen Victoria's Grandchildren. Those three monarchs were also distant relatives of the Belgian, Portuguese, and Bulgarian royal families. By the end of the war, most of Europe's royal dynasties

were kicked out of power, giving way to democratic leaders.

141) Germany used Zeppelin Airships to bomb several British cities, including London during WWI. The British town of Great Yarmouth was the first to be aerially bombarded by German Zeppelins. This happened on 19th January, 1915. Even though the airships moved slowly, they were hard to shoot down because they flew so high, beyond the reach of most British aircraft. Fortunately, the British developed the Sopwith Camel fighters which could shoot down the zeppelins. In total, the Germans dropped 280 tons of bombs in Britain during fifty three Zeppelin raids and deployed fifty two fixed wind airplane raids. They killed 1,413 civilians and wounded 3,409 more.

Zeppelin L 13

142) The British Royal Navy developed the first depth charges in the summer of 1916. This was an important game-changer in the war because, for the first time, they

were able to target and destroy German submarines which had been sinking most of their supply ships.

143) WWI caused a steel shortage and, as a result, many countries had to construct concrete ships.

144) More than 170 million rounds of shells were manufactured in Europe by the end of WWI.

145) Journalists were banned from the frontline during the war because most governments believed that reporting on the war would be beneficial to the enemy. Journalists who tried to report on the realities of war faced imprisonment or even execution.

146) A German navy captain named Karl Von Muller spared many civilian lives during WWI. He was ordered to sink allied merchant ships, which he did. However, on his own initiative, he would give passengers enough time to collect their belongings and to abandon the ships, before he would sink them.

147) The Pool of Peace in Belgium is one of the most well-known WWI memorials. Before the war, the Spanbroekmolen Windmill stood at that location for 300 years. In November 1914, the windmill was destroyed by Germans, and it became the site of many battles. The Germans held onto it, until June 1917, when the British exploded mines below the site, creating a crater, forty feet deep and 250 feet wide. The crater was filled with water, and it became the Pool of Peace.

148) Even though all fighting ceased by the end of 1918, technically, WWI didn't officially end until June 28, 1919, when the treaty of Versailles was signed.

149) Different countries had different nicknames for the helmets that were issued to them during the war. British soldiers called them 'Tin Hats' or 'Tommy', while American soldiers called them 'Doughboy', and German soldiers called them 'Salad Bowls'.

150) Food prices were so high during the war that the British government had to fix maximum food prices to ensure that people could afford to eat. There were also serious fuel shortages in Britain during the war and newspapers constantly printed advisories on how to save fuel when cooking.

151) Arthur Zimmerman, German's Foreign Minister during WWI, wrote a telegram to Mexico asking the country to join the war, and promising them territories within US soil if Germany won. Britain intercepted the telegram, decoded it, and later shared it with the US. This helped to convince America to join the war.

152) A British diplomat and a military officer named Thomas Edward Lawrence played a key role in engineering the Arab Revolt against the Turks. In the west, he became known as Lawrence of Arabia because he adopted Arabian culture so much that he looked more like an Arab than an Englishman.

153) In response to food and supply shortages during WWI, the British government criminalized certain things that were part of everyday life during peacetime. People

weren't allowed to sell candy and chocolate, to throw rice at weddings, or to sell cattle or horses.

154) The women who worked in factories that manufactured TNT in Britain were exposed to the toxic substance, and they suffered from jaundice. As a result of the jaundice, their skin turned orange-yellow, and they were nicknamed 'canary girls' or 'munitionettes'. 25% of all the canary girls died as a direct result of the toxins they handled at work.

155) A Hungarian soldier was shot in the brain (the frontal lobe area) during WWI. He survived, but he was physically unable to fall asleep. He lived his whole life without ever sleeping again.

156) When Adolf Hitler was a young soldier during WWI, he used to have a full moustache. He was however ordered by a senior German official to reduce it so that he could properly wear a gas mask. That's how he ended up with his iconic partial moustache.

157) After WWI, so many German men had died, that only one-third of women in the country were able to find husbands.

158) A compassionate British soldier spared the life of a wounded German during WWI. That man turned out to be Adolf Hitler.

159) Some children even served in the military during WWI with the youngest soldier to serve being only eight years old.

160) British soldiers drank so much tea during WWI, that at some point the military enforced rations of six pints of tea per soldier per day.

Soldiers having tea

161) Military commanders often sent orders to the battlefront by putting notes in capsules that were tied around dogs. The dogs would then run to the battlefront to deliver the orders.

162) As a result of WWI, the Women's Suffrage Movement in Britain was split into two. The Mainstream Suffragette Movement called for a ceasefire for the duration of the war (meaning they would not push for their demands until the war was over). The Radical Suffragette Movement chose to continue pushing for women's rights even during the war, and they even demanded that women in the military should be put in combat roles.

163) The war led to the empowerment of nationalists in British territories, especially after the concept of self-determination was introduced in Eastern Europe. The British

Empire faced resistance in Ireland, Egypt, India, Palestine, and Iraq towards the end of WWI.

164) The Belgian royal family had a very hands-on approach during the war. The King personally led the Belgian Army in battle, the Queen became a nurse and attended to wounded soldiers, and the Prince, who was only fourteen at the time, joined the army and served as a private.

165) Spain stayed neutral throughout WWI. Towards the end of the war, it was the only country whose media could freely report on the influenza epidemic. Other countries restricted such reports to maintain morale during the war. As a result, people thought that the country was more adversely affected by the flu, so they named it the Spanish Flu.

166) A British POW (prisoner of war) was in a German prison camp when he heard that his mother was dying. He pleaded with the Germans to let him go home and see his mother one last time, promising that he would come back. The German Kaiser let him go, expecting to never see him again. However, after visiting his ailing mother, the soldier actually did return to the prison camp.

167) After English, German was the second most-spoken language in the US before WWI. In fact, many schools, and local governments considered German an official language. However, when the war broke out, the language was suppressed, German books were burned, and German newspapers were discontinued in America.

168) During cold nights in the trenches, British and French soldiers would make 'machine gun tea'. They would put water into their machine guns, and fire thousands of rounds towards the German trenches. The water in the machine gun would boil in the process and the soldiers would then collect it and use it to brew tea.

169) The renowned French scientist Marie Curie tried to donate her Nobel Prize gold medals towards the war effort, but the French National Bank wouldn't take them.

170) RMS Olympic (a cruise liner and the sister ship to the Titanic) was the only civilian ship to ever destroy a German Submarine during WWI. The submarine tried to sink the Olympic, but the massive ship was able to ram into the submarine and sink it first.

171) Retired US president Teddy Roosevelt volunteered to join the army during WWI. His act of courage inspired many young men to sign up as well.

172) Germany used up all the rubber within its borders during the war. The post-war rubber shortages were so severe that Germans had to design bicycles with metal springs in place of rubber tires.

173) New Zealand, which was a British Dominion during WWI, raised an army of 100,000 soldiers who sailed to Europe to join the war. At the time, the country only had a population of 1 million, meaning that 10% of all New Zealanders fought in WWI.

174) During WWI, German submarines were such a serious threat, that at one point, the British Army tried to

train seagulls to target the submarines, and to poop on their periscopes. This plan failed because unlike pigeons, seagulls couldn't be trained.

German U-boat UB 14 with its crew

175) The legendary magician Houdini was hired by the US Army to teach the troops magic skills that could help them survive the war (like how to escape if they were captured and chained).

176) People with eye cataracts were hired to help detect flashing beacons of UV light during WWI. Some cataract patients tend to be very sensitive to ultraviolet light, and this came in handy when the allies were trying to land planes in the dark without being seen by the Germans.

177) Sexually transmitted diseases were very common during the war. When allied troops went home after the war, over 1.5 million cases of gonorrhoea and syphilis were reported in Britain, America and France.

178) King Edward VIII, who was the Prince of Wales at the time, wanted to join the army, but the government

wouldn't let him because they didn't want the heir to the throne dying in battle, or getting captured by the enemy. Edward VIII still visited the Western Front as often as he could, and he even earned the Military Cross for his role in the war. He was very well-liked by WWI veterans.

179) A thousand of London's iconic double-decker busses were used in the frontlines of WWI, mostly to ferry nurses and wounded soldiers to and from the trenches.

180) During WWI, the American navy painted its ships in dazzle camouflage (complex patterns of geometrical shapes). This was meant to create an optical illusion that would make it hard for the enemy to estimate how far the ships were, how fast they were moving, and in what direction they were headed.

181) During WWI, German and Russian soldiers were battling it out when they were all attacked by a pack of wolves. They agreed to a temporary ceasefire so that they could all deal with the wolves first.

182) Censorship was widely practiced by the British Government during WWI. For example, when the British vessel HMS Audacious was sunk in October 1914, the British Press was barred from reporting the incident. British citizens only found out about it through rumours spread by passengers who had witnessed the incident while aboard a different ship.

183) When the war broke out, cavalry units (horse riders) were considered superior to guard units (soldiers who marched on foot). In fact, members of cavalry regiments held higher military ranks than guardsmen. However,

armies on both sides of the conflict quickly realized that riding horses into the battlefield wasn't practical anymore because they could be mowed down by machine guns. From that point on, horses were only used for transport, not for charging into battle. Mules and horses were more reliable than lorries and tanks when it came to moving munitions through harsh terrain up to the battlefront during WWI.

184) Before WWI, Germany had set up a robust horse breeding program all over its empire. In fact, all horses had to be registered every year, as if they were members of the military reserves. That way, it was easy for the German Army to find enough horses when they were needed for battle. Britain didn't have as many horses as Germany but it imported one million horses from America during WWI. It also brought in an unconfirmed number of horses from New Zealand. Soldiers on both sides of the war made improvised gas masks and nose plugs to protect their horses from gas attacks during WWI, but the horses would mistake the masks for feed bags and destroy them, and they would end up dying anyway. Just like humans, horses would also get shell shocked during the war. Soldiers discovered that poorly bred horses would react bravely to the sound of exploding artillery, while well-bred horses would react in a cowardly manner. Historians estimate that horse lives were more valuable than human lives at some point during the war. In 1917, men who fell in battle could be replaced with new soldiers, but horses were irreplaceable.

Bazentin Ridge 1916

185) The British Government capitalized on Germany's attacks on civilians in order to encourage its citizens to join the army. British propaganda posters were used to argue that it was better to face bullets at the battlefront than to stay at home and be killed by bombs.

186) The French decided to build a 'fake Paris' near the actual city in order to confuse German bombers during WWI. Germany had been sending bombers to British cities in the dead of night, and the French were concerned that the same would happen in their country, so they decided to build entire neighborhoods that were imitations of Paris. The plan was to design 'fake Paris' in such a way that German pilots couldn't tell the difference when it was dark.

187) Sixteen days before the ill-fated civilian vessel RMS Lusitania set sail from America to Britain, Germany published an article in the New York Times, warning that it would sink the ship if it sailed as planned. The warning was ignored, and in the end, 1,198 lives were lost.

188) Women joined the police force in Britain for the first time during WWI. Initially, their jobs involved monitoring

other women working in munitions factories and helping to maintain discipline among the ranks. They also served as safety inspectors in the factories. Soon, they started patrolling public areas (e.g. train stations) and after the war, they became permanent police officers. Similarly, the transport sector in Britain was mostly staffed by women during the war. They worked as drivers, ticket collectors, cleaners and porters.

189) During WWI, there were special laws put in place for British civilians in military courts if they broke special rules that were created to help the war effort. People who were caught wasting food, selling strong alcohol, opening pubs past curfew time, wasting food by feeding wild animals, etc., could be brought before a military court and sentenced.

190) After the start of WWI, British women pushed for their own uniformed service. The WAAC (Women's Army Auxiliary Corps) was established during WWI, in December 1916. This paved the way for the creation of the Women's Royal Navy in 1917 and the Women's Royal Air force in 1918. In total, more than 100,000 women served in the British Military by the end of WWI.

191) A female Scottish doctor named Elsie Inglis volunteered to join the army as a medic when the war started. The military officers found her offer amusing, and told her to: "go home and sit still." She founded the Scottish Women's Hospital, and later, she moved to Serbia to treat wounded soldiers.

192) Women's soccer became popular during WWI. For the first time, women were working together in large numbers in factories, so they decided to engage in leisure activities that were previously reserved for men. Each munitions factory formed its own football team, and the matches drew massive crowds.

193) WWI trenches were layered. There were frontline trenches which were followed by two or more support trenches. They were linked by alleyways which were called communications trenches. Soldiers fought and kept watch in the frontline trenches. The support trenches were used to prepare food, treat wounded soldiers, and to store munitions.

194) Britain had limited detention policies during the war, where citizens of Germany, Austria, Hungary, and other "enemy" states had to register with the police and report to stations for regular checks. These people were also subject to several other restrictions. They couldn't travel, live in areas that were likely to be invaded, or own any equipment that could be used to spy on the British military.

195) During the war, the Maxim machine guns used in the trenches were operated by five people at a time. One man would sight the machine gun, the second man would fire, a third man would feed ammunition to the gun, and two others would go back and forth, bringing boxes of ammunition to the front and taking empty boxes away.

Firing a Maxim gun at an aeroplane

196) Artillery guns were never placed at the frontline trench. They were actually placed behind the second trench line (also known as the first support trench), meaning that they fired shells over the heads of soldiers. This contributed to a higher rate of shellshock among soldiers on both sides of the war.

197) The German public didn't always support the war. In fact, in 1918, citizens started demonstrating and striking, calling an end to the war. Many of them were starving and their economy was a mess, so they didn't see the benefit of being at war.

198) Despite the grim nature of WWI, nine out of ten British soldiers actually survived the war.

199) The British army had many 'pals' battalions' during WWI. These were battalions that were made up almost entirely of people who came from a small geographical area (same town, same place of work, etc.). Many soldiers joined such battalions because they didn't want their friends, neighbors, or former colleagues to think less of them.

200) Most British military personnel were posted outside Britain when WWI started. They were mostly tasked with keeping order in the territories of the vast British Empire (including India and the African and Asian Colonies).

201) Army generals were actually banned from fighting during the war. Before WWI, generals would ride into battle with their men, and this showed that they were brave and capable leaders. However, with the widespread use of machine guns, the military didn't want to put highly experienced generals at the battlefront because they didn't want to lose good strategists.

202) Plastic surgery was first introduced during WWI. Surgeons started using skin grafts to repair the faces of victims who had suffered serious facial injuries.

203) In the years leading up to the war, Britain had a 'Two-Power Standard' for its naval fleet (which was the best in the world at that time). Under this standard, the Royal Navy was required to have a number of battleships whose collective strength was at least, equal to the combined strength of the second and third strongest navies in the world (which were France and Russia).

204) Two billion letters and an additional 114 million parcels were sent through the Royal Mail Service during the war. On average, twelve million letters were sent and delivered to and from the front every single week. Letters were the primary form of long-distance communication at the time, and the British army believed that keeping in touch with family members boosted soldiers' morale.

205) In the days leading up to the war, there was widespread public unrest in Britain (and even more so in Ireland). Suffrage and labor movements were initially opposed to the war. However, most movements quickly rallied behind the government, when it became clear that winning the war was a matter of national pride.

206) During WWI, Britain was in 'total war' for the first time in its history. Total war meant that all public resources (both civilian and military) were directed towards fighting the enemy. It also meant that civilians could be ordered by the government to do certain things to support the war effort. For example, private steel millers were required to work for the government to make weapons.

207) Britain had a special 'war cabinet' during WWI. Its function was to make sure that government resources were utilized efficiently during the war, and that the war effort wasn't undermined by endless administrative red tape.

208) Motorized ambulances were created during the first war out of necessity and thousands volunteered to be drivers, including the famous Walt Disney.

WWI field ambulance vehicle

209) Catholic bishops were opposed to compulsory enlistment into the army, and they called for their church members to oppose the policy. This had a significant impact in Ireland (which was, and remains largely Catholic), and it may have contributed to the eventual withdrawal of Ireland from the UK.

210) WWI had a lasting effect on Britain's internal politics. The Conservative Party was credited with winning the war, while the liberal party was criticized for being indecisive (their leadership was seen as weak) during the war.

211) During peacetime, before the war, the British government only spent 13% of the country's GNP (Gross National Product), but the number increased greatly during the war, and by 1918, the government was spending up to 59% of Britain's GNP. Additionally, the government borrowed heavily, imposed heavy taxes, cancelled virtually all projects that weren't war-related, and diverted funds from other public services. Within the

duration of the war, British public debt rose from £625 million to £7.8 billion in less than five years.

212) In 1916, the government of Britain made it illegal for anyone dining in a public establishment to eat more than two courses for lunch and more than three courses for supper. Because times were hard, everyone was required to 'tighten their belts'.

213) The British royal family had to change its family name from 'The House of Saxe-Coburg and Gotha' to 'The House of Windsor' to appease the British public who were unhappy with the royal family's German ancestry. The British royals also dropped all their German titles and names and took up English surnames. German relatives of British royals who fought in the war had their titles stripped from them under the rules outlined in the Titles Deprivation Act of 1917. They were no longer considered to be in line for the British Crown.

214) By 1917, Britain consumed 827 million barrels of oil per year, most of which were shipped from the United States (and some from Mexico).

215) When the Russians revolted and overthrew Tsar Nicholas II, the Russian Government wanted him to be given asylum in Britain. The British cabinet agreed to offer the Tsar and his family asylum, but King George V (who was the Tsar's first cousin), felt that the public wouldn't like it, so he blocked the asylum offer. The Tsar and his family were later killed.

216) Most of the fighting during WWI occurred in Belgium, France, Luxembourg, and Alsace-Lorraine (a

part of modern-day France). These areas were at the heart of the war, although smaller related conflicts and resultant battles were spread across the world.

217) Germany officially joined WWI to back up Austria-Hungary, but behind the scenes, those in power saw the war as an opportunity to settle scores and disputes with other European powers (France, Russia, and Britain). Colonial disputes in Africa (and some parts of Asia) played a minor role in starting WWI. Although European powers had subdivided most of Africa and agreed on colonial boundaries, there were still some unresolved tensions because the Germans thought France and Britain had taken larger parts of the continent.

218) France had a big and war-ready army at the start of WWI because it had 'universal conscription'. Every year, men who were about to turn twenty one were enlisted into the army, and they served in active duty for three years before going into the reserves. It was therefore very easy for the French to mobilize a massive army on short notice because most able-bodied men were already trained, and they were either in active service or in the reserves.

219) In August 1914, after suffering a series of devastating losses, the French feared that Paris would fall, so they moved the government to Bordeaux.

220) The French had a tradition of firing or transferring Generals and Commanders-in-chief who lost in battle. This practice had mixed results during WWI. In some cases, it led to better performance, but in others, it led to greater losses.

221) In 1917, many in the French army had completely lost morale for the war. They had come to believe that their infantry units would never prevail against German artillery and superior machine guns. They believed that they were dying in vain, and France would fall anyway. Their greatest hope was the arrival of American soldiers. In the spring of 1917, over 35,000 French soldiers mutinied. Most of these cases were the result of disappointment and despair among the soldiers. Their latest offensive (the Neville offensive) had failed. They were expecting backup from American soldiers who had not shown up. The mutinies were kept secret for the remainder of the war, because the French government worried that these cases would spread.

222) During WWI, French soldiers fought in other theaters of war apart from the Western Front. France sent some soldiers to occupy German colonies in Cameroon and Togo, and others to fight against the Ottomans in Palestine and the Dardanelles. The French also used troops from their North African territories and other colonies to fight in secondary battles, so as to avoid diverting too many soldiers from the Western Front. These troops were used to fight in Romania and in the Balkans.

223) When Germany was defeated, the allies took away Cameroon, Togo, and Tanganyika as part of the post-war settlements.

224) Rifle designs remained the same throughout WWI because all countries were focused on improving their larger weapons (such as tanks and machine guns), and developing chemical weapons (poisonous gases).

Machine gun crew with gas masks

225) France suffered mass casualties at the start of WWI partly because they were trained to attack the enemy in mass formations, a strategy that was outdated by that time (because the Germans had machine guns). The fact that their soldiers wore blue uniforms that were easily visible by enemy soldiers, also didn't help.

226) The German homeland was safe for most of the war, with the exception of the East Prussia region, which was temporarily invaded by the Russians in 1914. Other than that, there were virtually no battles fought within Germany in the entire war.

227) The German monarchy had hoped that the war would unite people behind the Kaiser and lessen the public support for the Social Democrats (who were critical of the monarchy). This worked at first as the Social Democrats backed the Kaiser, but when the war took longer than expected, Germans became unhappy again. After their defeat, the Germans were discontent with their government, and they had a revolution between

1918 and 1919. As a result of the revolution, they kicked out their monarchs and embraced a stronger democratic system. As the war ended, the German Kaiser (and his heirs) stepped down from the throne and the Social Democratic Party formed a government. The German Empire fell, and it was replaced by the Weimar Republic.

228) In 1915, the German government massacred five million pigs in an incident that came to be known as 'Schweinemord'. The pigs were killed both for food, and as a way to reserve more grains (which were used as pig feed).

229) When the Belgians were invaded by the Germans (whose ultimate aim was to get to France), they resisted the invasion by fighting back and destroying their own railways to keep the Germans from advancing. Germans had expected to have an easy passage through Belgium, so they angrily reacted by killing 6,000 civilians.

230) After America declared war on Germany, some German generals didn't see it as much of a threat because they believed that Americans were fat, undisciplined, and unfamiliar with the hardships of prolonged severe fighting. They were however disappointed to discover that American soldiers were in good form and highly motivated to win the war.

231) In 1916, Germany implemented the Hindenburg Program, which required that all economic resources in the country be put towards the creation of weapons. Church bells, copper roofs, and many other metal installa-

tions were ripped out, taken to munitions factories, and used as raw materials.

232) In Germany, only soldiers who were permanently crippled could be discharged from the army. Wounded soldiers were sent back to the trenches as soon as they showed signs of recovery.

Wounded soldiers at Omaha Beach

233) Soldiers on both sides of the war were issued with rifles. British soldiers used the Lee-Enfield .303 bolt-action rifle during WWI and its standard magazine could hold ten bullets. It was a well-made weapon that performed well under the tough conditions in the trenches. German infantry soldiers used the Gewehr 98 rifle. It was well designed and fairly accurate, but it wasn't well suited for the trenches.

234) Machine guns were very important in determining the outcomes of many battles in WWI. The Germans used the Maschinengewehr 08, a variation of the original American Maxim machine gun. This gun could fire up to

400 rounds per minute. The British used the Vickers machine gun, which was also a Maxim machine gun variant. It could fire 450 to 500 rounds per minute.

235) There were many different types of artillery guns used during the war. Artillery was meant to 'soften up' enemy positions before the infantry teams could advance. The British used the Howitzer Mark 1, which could fire two shells a minute (each weighing 290 pounds/131kg). The Germans had the so-called 'Paris Gun' which they famously used to shell Paris from 75 miles (120 km) away. It could fire shells up to 25 miles (40 km) into the air. Most of the shells fired from the 'Paris gun' never actually hit the city, but they were so loud they scared many civilians into evacuating.

236) When WWI started, most armies had small planes with bodies made of wood and canvas. By the end of the war, they had highly sophisticated fighters like the German Fokker Eindecker and the British Sopwith Camel. Most historians agree that the aviation industry wouldn't have advanced so much in the early 20th century if WWI hadn't happened.

237) In response to Germans using U-boats (submarines) to sink merchant ships, the British built 'Q-Ships'. These were battleships that were disguised as merchant ships. They would wait for German submarines to emerge before shooting and destroying them. When German submarines switched to torpedoing merchant ships without emerging from the water, the British started using convoys to secure their supply ships. Battleships would

meet merchant ships at sea and escort them till they docked on British shores.

238) European powers that participated in WWI evaluated an estimated 3,000 chemicals for potential use as weapons. Of those, fifty were actually used on the battlefield.

239) In Flanders (a place in northern Belgium), it's estimated that one million miles (1.61 million kilometers) of barbed wire was used at the battlefront. That's enough barbed wire to circle the earth about forty times over.

240) The shells used during WWI were unreliable; a significant percentage would remain unexploded after being launched. It's estimated that there are still millions of unexploded WWI shells buried in the French countryside even today. Records show that every single year, bomb disposal units handle about forty tons of unexploded shells within the Verdun area of France alone.

241) Battlefield tactics evolved in many ways during WWI. For example, at the start of the war, commanders were in charge of companies with more than 100 men. By the end of the war, commanders were in charge of squads of about ten soldiers or so.

242) When Germans first used chlorine gas in battle, allied soldiers thought that it was just a smoke-screen meant to provide cover for German soldiers who were about to attack. They marched onward into the cloud of chlorine gas, and many of them were killed.

243) Poison gases proved to be very unreliable weapons during the war. They were double-edged swords. Attackers who used the gas were often killed when the winds shifted and blew in the opposite direction. To deal with this problem, the Germans developed special artillery shells that could be used to deliver poison gas to enemy positions.

244) When the war started, generals would use motorcycle couriers to deliver orders from command stations to the battlefront. This method became ineffective because battle conditions would change so rapidly. They, therefore, changed tactics and started using mirrors and flashing lights to send orders in Morse code. In some cases, fast runners would deliver more detailed messages. As the war went on, both sides started using aircraft to drop messages from generals to the soldiers at the battlefront.

245) Both the allies and the Germans floated manned observation balloons above the trenches. The balloons were used as observation posts. They were manned by two soldiers who would observe enemy positions and send messages down to the artillery operators. Enemy planes would often try to shoot down the balloons, but they were protected by anti-aircraft guns on the ground.

Observation balloon ascending

246) In the early stages of WWI, pilots used to go up without any parachutes. That's mostly because the kinds of parachutes that were available at the time were too heavy to bring along. Britain was slow in developing lighter parachutes because they were concerned that if pilots had parachutes, they would become cowards and abandon their planes at the first sight of trouble.

247) Large bomber aircrafts were developed in the course of WWI. These bombers would fly deep into enemy territory and drop bombs on strategic sites (mostly supply bases). The bombers were slow easy targets, so they had to fly along with many fighter escorts for protection.

248) The Germans were the first to train and deploy snipers who used rifles with telescopic sights to shoot allied soldiers who exposed themselves in the trenches.

249) As European countries were taking sides at the start of the war, Spain's Prime Minister Eduardo Dato declared that Spain would remain neutral. This declaration was

made on August 7, 1914, and it stayed in place for the entire duration of the war.

250) Japan participated in WWI, in alliance with the allies (Britain, France, and Russia). Japan was tasked with securing shipping lanes in the Pacific and the Indian Ocean, to keep them from falling under the control of Germany. The Japanese had imperial ambitions during WWI and they saw the war as an opportunity to expand their influence in China and other Asian countries. Since Germany was busy fighting the war, Japan seized some German territories in and around Asia (e.g. Micronesia). Although Japan and the United States fought on the same side during WWI, there was a lot of tension between the two powers throughout that era. The US was opposed to Japan's ambitions to colonize Asian countries, and they even blocked Japan's plans to send 70,000 troops to occupy Siberia in 1918. Japan was also concerned about America's increasing influence in Asia.

PART II
WORLD WAR II

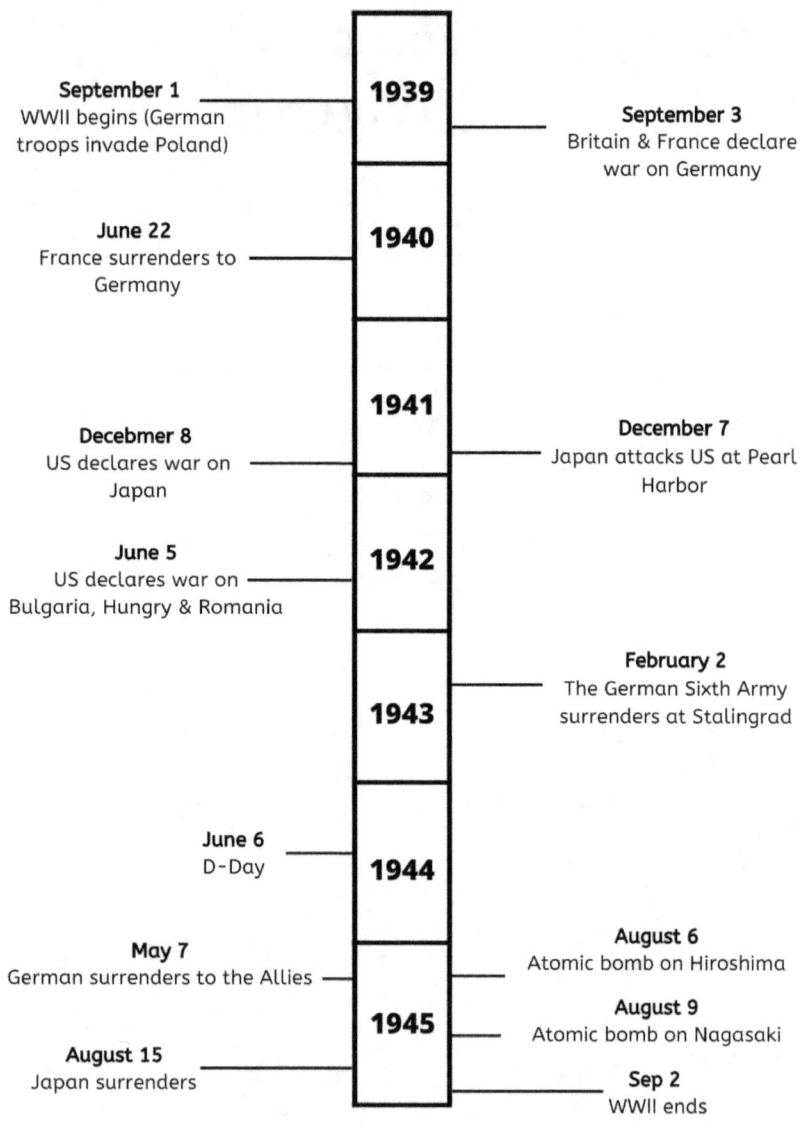

WWII FACTS

1) Throughout the 1930s, in the lead up to WWII, Nazi Germany engaged in a quick process of rearmament (building up of military resources) in violation of the conditions outlined in the Treaty of Versailles that ended WWI, and several other agreements. They also formed alliances with like-minded countries (e.g. Japan and Italy) and were getting ready for war.

2) In the lead up to WWII, France and Britain were trying their best to avoid another European war, so, as it became increasingly clear that Germany was hoping for war, the two allies remained committed to their policy of appeasement (going out of their way to avoid confrontation). There were some in France and Britain who wanted the allies to take the Nazi German threat more seriously, but the official position was to try to avoid doing anything that could anger the Germans and start a war.

3) WWII is officially considered to have started on September 1, 1939. The starting date of WWII is however

not universally agreed upon. Some historians argue that WWII started with the Second Sino-Japanese war (in July 1937) when war broke out between Japanese Imperialists and Chinese Revolutionaries at the Marco Polo Bridge. Others even believe that the war started way back in September 1931 when Japan invaded Manchuria.

4) On the 23rd of August, 1939, Germany and the Soviet Union signed a pact that clearly stated which Eastern and Central European countries fell within either of their spheres of influence. That pact cleared the way for German's invasion of Poland. Since Poland fell within Germany's sphere of influence according to the pact, it meant that the Soviets wouldn't intervene after Germany invaded the country. On September 1st, 1939, the Nazis invaded Poland.

5) Britain had promised to guarantee Poland's sovereignty (right to be a free country) after Hitler took over Czechoslovakia and people were worried that he would do the same with other small European countries. When the Nazis invaded Poland, Britain weighed its options, and two days later, on September 3rd 1939, they declared war on Germany.

6) The London air was filled with the sound of sirens minutes after British Prime Minister Neville Chamberlain finished his War Declaration speech. The sirens were meant to warn British citizens to take shelter in case German air raids were incoming.

7) The German invasion of Poland in September and October of 1939 resulted in the loss of many Polish lives.

70,000 polish fighters were killed and 133,000 injured. An estimated 45,000 civilians were killed in cold blood during the initial invasion and 700,000 citizens were taken as POW (prisoners of war).

German troops parade through Warsaw

8) The Soviet Union invaded Poland sixteen days after Germany did the same. The battle that followed led to the loss of 50,000 Polish lives. The USSR went into Poland under the alleged reason that the Polish State did not exist anymore, so its territory was up for grabs.

9) After declaring war on Germany, in September 1939, Britain adopted a non-aggression strategy. It involved the use of propaganda material in an attempt to influence public opinion in Germany. The Royal Air Force would drop leaflets in Germany, urging people to resist Nazi policies. Britain also hoped that by dropping pamphlets deep into German airspace, the Nazis would see how easy it would be for Britain to bomb them, and that would serve as a warning.

10) The Soviets tried to invade Finland between November and December 1939. Their troops were however defeated, and the USSR was thrown out of the League of Nations. The Soviets made a second attempt to invade Finland in March of 1940, and this time they managed to get the Finns to sign a peace treaty with them, giving them control over some areas in Finland.

11) Germans used military tactics popularly known as Blitzkrieg. They involved the use of armoured trucks and aircraft to rapidly move deep into enemy territory. That way, they would manage to gain control over vast areas even before the opposing army had time to strategize and mount a proper defence.

12) In the wake of WWI, France had constructed the Maginot Line. This was a special wall that was lined with heavy weaponry, and manned by soldiers around the clock. It was made to protect France from the Germans. However, when Germany invaded France during WWII, they chose to avoid the Maginot Line altogether, and instead, they came in through the Ardennes (in Luxembourg and Belgium). The French didn't build a fortified wall in that area because they assumed that the Germans would try to avoid the harsh landscape of the Ardennes. Germans were able to stream into France in large numbers after they broke through French defences in The Battle of Sedan (which was fought between 12-15 May in 1940). That was the beginning of the fall of France.

13) WWII ended on September 2nd, 1945. It lasted a total of 6 years and 1 day.

14) WWII was fought in Europe, the Pacific Ocean, the Atlantic Ocean, China, South East Asia, The Middle East, the Mediterranean, Australia, The North and the Horn of Africa, and briefly, in North and South America. It was fought between the Allied Powers and the Axis Powers. The Allied Powers included the Soviet Union, the United States, the United Kingdom, and China. The Axis Powers included Germany, The Japanese Empire, and the Italians.

15) WWII was fought under a state of "total war" (where the entire economy of a participating country is directed towards the war effort), and it involved more than thirty countries and 100 million combatants.

16) WWII is still the deadliest conflict in all of human history. It is estimated that between seventy million and eighty five million lives were lost during the conflict. The war included the holocaust, the use of nuclear weapons, the strategic use of starvation and disease to weaken entire countries, and the bombings of civilian populations.

17) Nationalists in Germany were unhappy with the treaty of Versailles (signed after WWI) where Germany lost a lot of territory and colonies and were forced to make financial restitution. This led to widespread anger and resentment in the country, which led to the rise of nationalist leaders like Hitler, who was Chancellor of Germany during WWII.

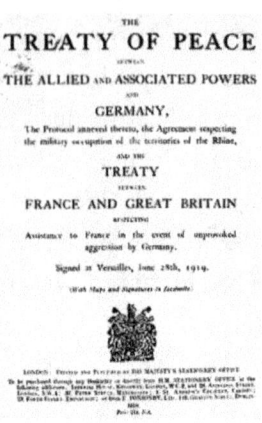

Treaty of Versailles

18) The League of Nations, which was in charge of keeping the peace between countries after WWI and before WWII, turned out to be a very weak organization. Countries would openly violate League of Nations rules without suffering any consequences. When the League of Nations tried to intervene in conflicts, some countries would just leave the organization. Japan left when the League of Nations spoke up against its decision to invade China.

19) Coming out of WWI, Italy was unhappy that Britain and France had not honored the promises they had made during the peace settlement. At the same time, fascism was on the rise in Italy, and that paved the way for Benito Mussolini who seized power and became the Italian leader, and Hitler's close ally during WWII. Leading up to WWII, Italy wanted to be a world power, and it pursued an aggressive foreign policy with the intention of creating a "New Roman Empire." Italy had always wanted to have Ethiopia as a colony. It invaded Ethiopia, and that resulted

in a war that lasted between 1935 and 1936. France and Britain did nothing to stop this invasion, even though it was a clear violation of the rules outlined by the League of Nations. This made Italy bold and more willing to violate other international laws.

20) Right before WWII, European powers were involved in a proxy war (a competition to see which country was more powerful) during the Spanish Civil War. Germany and Italy backed the nationalists in Spain, who were led by General Francisco Franco. The nationalists won. The USSR backed the existing Spanish Government which lost the Civil War. European powers used the Spanish Civil war to test out some of their new military technologies and strategies, which they ended up using during WWII.

21) The first official battle of WWII was the Battle of WesterPlatte, which was fought near the Polish Border with Germany.

22) When Poland fell, the Polish army surrendered to Germany in October of 1939, but the Polish government never did. Polish government officials fled the country and formed a "government in exile", which worked secretly with the allies in an attempt to regain control of Poland. That same month, the Western part of Poland was annexed by Germany, and the Eastern part was annexed by the Soviet Union. Some Polish territories were handed to Slovakia and Lithuania.

23) In 1939, Lithuania, Latvia, Estonia, and Finland were determined to be within the Soviet Union's sphere of

influence. The USSR ordered these countries to allow its troops to be stationed within their borders. All countries agreed, except Finland, and this led to the Finno-Soviet War.

24) Germany brought in a lot of iron ore from Sweden during WWII. In fact, it invaded both Norway and Denmark in 1940, just to protect its supply route from Sweden.

25) The British public was unhappy with Neville Chamberlain's leadership (especially after the Germans won control over Norway). As a result, Winston Churchill was appointed Prime Minister on May 10, 1940.

Winston Churchill as Prime Minister

26) Paris fell on the 14th of June, 1940. Italy had declared war on both Britain and France and it had invaded France on the 10th June, 1940. The French army was overwhelmed fighting both Germany and Italy, and that led to the fall of Paris. France signed a peace agreement with

Germany on the 22nd June, 1940. Under that agreement, France was occupied by both Germany and Italy. There was an area in France (the Vichy State) that was unoccupied by Axis forces, but it couldn't stand up against Germany, so it fell under their control.

27) After France fell, Britain tried to destroy French military equipment and resources to keep them from the hands of the German Military.

28) America had passed the Neutrality Act that was meant to keep it from joining any armed conflict in Europe, but in November 1939, it revised the Act and started to sell arms and other resources to the allies. To maintain the appearance of neutrality, the United States would let countries ship their own weapons across the Atlantic Ocean to Europe.

29) The Axis powers (Germany, Italy, and Japan) signed the Tripartite Pact in September, 1940. Under this pact, any country (with the exception of the Soviet Union) that would enter into war with one of the three countries, would effectively be at war with all of them. Slovakia, Hungary, and Romania joined the Axis powers in November, 1940, while Bulgaria and Yugoslavia joined later on in March, 1941. Yugoslavian opposition overthrew the government and opposed the decision to join the axis power, but Hitler invaded both Yugoslavia and Greece at the same time. By the end of May, 1941, all Balkan States were under the control of the Axis powers.

30) The Soviet Union considered joining the Axis powers in 1940, and they were in negotiations with Germany to

do so, but they couldn't agree on the terms. The soviets had many demands that threatened Germany's authority as the leader of the Axis Powers, so Hitler decided to invade the Soviets instead of making them allies.

31) WWII caused one of the most serious refugee crises in history. In the summer of 1940 alone, eight million Belgian, Dutch and French people were displaced from their homes, with nowhere to go.

32) In mid-1940, the British Royal Air force had 1,960 aircraft, while the German air force (the Luftwaffe) had over 2,500 aircrafts (including fighters, bombers, dive-bombers, coastal planes, and recon planes). This meant that by sheer numbers alone, the Germans had a stronger air force than the British during the early stages of WWII.

Royal Air Force Operation in the Far East

33) In 1940, the German air force bombed cities in Britain (mostly London) and it led to the loss of 40,000 civilian lives. This was known as the Blitz. London, in particular, was bombed continuously for fifty seven nights, starting September 7th, 1940. More than 180,000 people spent

their nights in underground shelters (mostly tunnels) in London.

34) The famous "Keep Calm and Carry On" posters were first issued by the British government in 1939 as the country prepared for WWII. It was one of a series of posters that were issued to cheer up and reassure the public who were worried about possible German air raids.

35) After the Germans bombarded British cities, there was rubble all over the British streets. The Government collected all that rubble and used it to construct runways for the Royal Air force. This showed that despite the grim circumstances, Britain had not lost its fighting spirit, and was willing to make the best of a bad situation.

36) The allied powers and axis powers fought hard for control of the Mediterranean. Between January and August of 1941 alone, ninety axis ships were sunk in the Mediterranean.

37) Hitler approved the euthanasia program in Germany to get rid of people who were seen as burdens to society. As a result, 100,000 Germans with physical disabilities or mental illnesses were murdered by August, 1941.

38) Control of oil supplies was very crucial during WWII. Both sides put a lot of effort into acquiring or keeping oil-rich territories. British and Soviet troops invaded Iran to take over its oil resources while German and Italian forces fought hard to retain control over Romanian oil fields.

39) In 1925, fourteen years before WWII, Adolf Hitler published a book (Mein Kampf) in which he expressed his

intention to invade other countries and put them under German control. Long before WWII, the Nazi leader already believed that war was necessary to secure the future wealth of Germany.

40) The Nazis used hunger as a war strategy. Under the "Nazi Hunger Plan", more than two million soviet prisoners were literally starved to death in 1941.

41) After the Germans took over Poland, they rounded up all mentally handicapped Polish citizens, and in November, 1939, they used chambers filled with carbon dioxide to kill all of them.

42) When the Nazis rounded up and detained or murdered Jews and people of other ethnicities, they would take their possessions and reuse them. Valuable items would be given to soldiers as gifts, clothes would be given to Germans who needed them, and metallic items would be used as raw material to make weapons.

43) An estimated total of six million Jews were killed in the holocaust during WWII. It's estimated that about two million Jews living in the Western Soviet Union were murdered and buried in mass graves between 1941 and 1944, in what was known as the "holocaust by bullets."

The holocaust in Poland

44) Otto Kretschmer, a German Naval commander, is considered the most prolific submariner of WWII. He was responsible for sinking thirty seven allied ships. He was captured by the British royal navy in March of 1941.

45) As WWII went on, Americans wanted to lend material support to the allies without really joining the war. As a result, the Senate passed a Lend-Lease Bill which allowed the United States to loan war machinery and supplies to the allies, which they would pay back after the war.

46) 60% of all Japanese soldiers who died during WWII lost their lives due to malnutrition and resultant diseases.

47) The Americans bombed Iwo Jima Island for seventy six days before they sent in an assault fleet of about 30,000 marines to invade the island.

48) The US, Britain, and several other Western nations put an oil embargo (restriction) on Japan after it invaded Indo-China in July, 1941. This greatly limited Japan's military capabilities. Japan was planning to invade the Soviet

Union from the East, but it put off those plans because of the oil restriction.

49) Japan's WWII strategy involved grabbing all European colonies in Asia so that they could exploit resources from those colonies and use the land as a defensive perimeter, creating some distance between their homeland and the nearest European armies. Throughout the war, Japan planned to neutralize America's fleet in the pacific because it wanted to be the sole power in the Asia-pacific region.

50) When the US, UK, Australia, and China declared war on Japan, the Soviet Union (even though it was one of the allies) still maintained a neutrality agreement that it had in place with Japan.

51) On the 1st of January, 1942, the main allies, together with twenty two other governments (including some governments in exile) agreed to implement the Atlantic Charter. The countries agreed that none of them would sign a separate peace deal with the Axis powers. This ensured that the allies weren't weakened by some countries leaving the war before they had totally won (like Russia did in WWI).

52) Even though all allied powers agreed that defeating Germany was their biggest priority, they had different preferences when it came to strategy. For example, in 1942, the Americans thought that a direct large scale attack through France would be the best approach. The British wanted a war of attrition (where they would attack Germany on the outer edges of their territory, and wear them out over time). The Soviets thought that starting a

second front would strain German resources (at this point, they were the only ones fighting Germans on land at the Eastern front).

53) Japan was able to conquer many Asian and pacific territories by May, 1942. With the help of Thailand, they conquered Malaya, the Dutch East Indies, Burma, Rabaul, and Singapore. They were also able to capture the Philippine Commonwealth, despite tough resistance from America and Filipino soldiers. Japan had many easy victories over countries and territories that weren't prepared for war. As a result, they became overconfident, and they over-extended their army, making them vulnerable.

54) The ability to intercept enemy messages and to break their code was an important part of WWII. It determined the outcomes of many battles, for example, Americans broke Japanese naval codes, and as a result, they were able to win the Midway Battle (it was called the Midway Battle because it was in the pacific, halfway between America and Japan).

Battle of Midway- An unexpected victory

55) Four out of five German soldiers who lost their lives during WWII, died in the Eastern Front, fighting the Soviets.

56) Before the swastika was a symbol for Nazi Germany, it used to be an ancient symbol for good fortune and fertility in several Eastern religious traditions (including Hinduism and Buddhism).

57) In response to Hitler's treatment of Jews in Europe, more than 600,000 American Jews joined the US armed forces and fought in WWII.

58) For the entire duration of the war, the allies dropped over 3.4 million tons of bombs. That's roughly 27,700 tons every single month for six continuous years.

59) The Japanese "Kamikaze" war strategy was created as a way to balance out America's technological advantage during WWII. It involved filling planes with explosives and letting pilots fly them on a suicide mission into American military establishments. An estimated three

thousand Japanese pilots took part in the Kamikaze attacks.

60) Japan used "wind ship weapons" to target America. They launched about 9,000 balloons that carried bombs, and sent them to different destinations in America. This mission generally failed because only a thousand balloons hit their targets, and only six people died as a result of the attack.

61) It's estimated that 1.5 million children were killed in the holocaust. The vast majority of them were Jewish children, but tens of thousands of Gypsy children were also murdered.

62) The USSR had the highest number of casualties in WWII. It's estimated that it lost twenty one million people in total.

63) The concentration camps were so bad that even after the Jewish detainees were liberated from these camps, thousands of them died later on as a result of the conditions they were subjected to in the camps. Between the Bergen-Belsen and Dachau camps, more than 15,000 detainees died within six weeks after being liberated.

64) The Nazis created a fictional person named Max Heiliger. They used his identity to open bank accounts that they used to launder the money and gold they had stolen from the Jews that were detained.

65) Before WWII, Europe had been the center of world power for centuries. After the war, European powers declined, and the US and USSR emerged as superpowers.

66) Radar was used for the first time by aviators in WWII. It was accidentally invented before the war by a British engineer who was trying to create a "death ray" to destroy enemy planes.

67) When British soldiers liberated the Bergen-Belsen camp in April, 1945, they had to burn it to the ground to contain the spread of typhus.

68) During WWII, American factories manufactured seven million rifles, three million machine guns, 650,000 jeeps, 300,000 aircraft, and 89,000 tanks. They were used by Americans as well as allied forces to win the war.

Military production during World War II

69) The Nazis performed lots of brutal medical experiments on Jewish detainees during WWII. In the name of research, they conducted several inhumane things including: hitting people's skulls with hammers to see how much pressure it would take for skulls to crack, repeatedly

breaking people's bones to see if the healing process would stop after several breaks, exposing men and women's reproductive organs to X-rays to see how different doses affected their ability to conceive or bear children, and amputating people to perform transplant experiments. The Nazis kept detailed records of their experiments, but today, it's considered unethical to use any of that material for reference purposes.

70) On January 20, 1942, at the Wannsee Conference in Berlin, Germany decided to implement the "Final Solution" that was proposed by a group led by Heinrich Himmler. The Jewish community was seen as a "problem" in Germany and some other fascist countries at the time, and the final solution meant the "extermination" of all Jews within German territory.

71) The bloodiest battle of WWII was the Battle of Stalingrad. It's also considered by many historians to be the bloodiest battle in human history. It lasted from 1942 to 1943, and anywhere between 800,000 and 1.6 million lives were lost.

Battle of Stalingrad

72) American military spending rose dramatically during WWII. In 1940, when America was still neutral, it had a defence budget of $1.9 billion. However, by 1945, military spending had shot up to $59.8 billion.

73) The SS (Schutzstaffel) was a powerful paramilitary organization in Germany during WWII. They started out as Hitler's personal guards, but they became the most influential and most feared group in all of Nazi Germany.

74) A German physicist named Hermann Oberth had the idea to build a space weapon for the Nazis. The concept involved putting a giant magnifying glass (which he referred to as the "sun-gun") in space and using it to concentrate the sun's beams and target them at important British and allied installations.

75) The Germans murdered Poles by the millions, but in the process, they noticed that Polish babies looked very similar to German babies. They decided to kidnap around 50,000 Polish babies and give them to German families so that they could be "Germanized."

76) The US military wanted to minimize its use of atomic bombs, but it already had several potential targets lined up. Had Japan not surrendered, Tokyo would have been the next city in Japan to be hit by an atomic bomb.

77) Germany had the strongest artillery gun of any nation that fought in the war. The artillery gun was named Karl, and it had the ability to shoot shells of up to 2.5 tons over a distance of three miles (five kilometers) and could burst through up to nine feet (three meters) of concrete. Karl was mostly used in wars against the USSR.

78) Adolf Hitler had a nephew named William Hitler who was an American citizen and served in the US Navy during the war. William Hitler changed his name after the war.

79) Germany was the first country to use jet fighters in WWII. Unfortunately for them, the jet fighters were made too late in the game to change the final outcome of the war.

80) Thousands of people in German-occupied territories risked their lives to save their Jewish friends and neighbors from the Nazis. Denmark managed to save its entire Jewish population. People like Oscar Schindler, Raoul Wallenberg, and Chiune Sugihara were in good standing with the Nazis, but still put their lives on the line to save as many Jews as they could.

81) During the Pearl Harbor attack, 2,402 Americans were killed, and another 1,280 were wounded. Eighteen out of ninety-six ships anchored at the harbor, and three hundred aircraft were either damaged, destroyed, or sunk.

82) When Germany was defeated, many of the most-wanted war criminals (mostly high ranking Nazi officers) hid in displaced person camps and pretended to be refugees. Many of them managed to get away and they were never brought to justice.

83) Japan had a large spy ring in North America during WWII. Contrary to popular belief, most Japanese spies were located in Mexico, not in the United States. They were mostly tasked with spying on America's Atlantic Fleet.

84) Eighty five percent of all POWs in Soviet camps ended up dying in the camps.

85) Some people in occupied European countries collaborated with the Nazis, either willingly or as a result of coercion. When these countries were liberated, some collaborators were shot or beaten by angry locals, and some female collaborators had their heads forcefully shaved.

86) The British military used balloons to protect population centers during air raids. The balloons were linked to networks of steel cables before they were left to drift upwards. This forced German bombers to fly higher to avoid the cables, and as a result, they were more likely to miss their targets.

87) After the Pearl Harbor raid, President Theodore Roosevelt realized that he needed a bulletproof car. At the time, the US Government had a $750 cap on how much taxpayers' money could be spent on a car. The president had to use an armoured limousine that the treasury

department had seized from notorious gangster Al Capone.

88) Nazis would identify themselves to each other with their "Heil Hitler" salute during WWII. Those who refused to do the salute were considered enemies of Germany.

89) During the blitzkrieg raids, German planes were fitted with sirens that sounded like loud screams. This was meant to terrify and psychologically torture the civilians in the targeted cities.

Strategic bombing during World War II

90) In 1938, the year before the start of WWII, Hitler was Time Magazine's Man of the year.

91) A twelve-year-old boy named Calvin Graham joined the US Navy. He was so brave in his service to the Navy that he was awarded a Purple Heart and a Bronze Star. The Navy only found out that he was a minor after the honors were already awarded.

92) Germany never actually declared war on any of the countries it invaded in Europe or Asia. In fact, the US is the only country on which Germany formally declared war during WWII.

93) Hitler believed that he was forming the third German Empire, also known as the "Third Reich." According to him, the Holy Roman Empire (of 962 to 1806) was the First Reich, the German Empire (of 1871 to 1918) was the Second Reich, and his Nazi Empire was therefore the Third Reich.

94) A Yugoslavian spy named Dusko Popov was able to get information that Japan planned to attack Pearl Harbor. He shared this information with the American government, but the FBI didn't take his warning seriously.

95) Two hundred Navajo Native Americans were enlisted in the US Marines as "code talkers" during WWII. They used the Navajo language as the basis for their code, and the Japanese weren't able to crack the code at all for the duration of the war.

96) All European and world powers had access to chemical weapons during WWII, but only Japan and Italy used such weapons in battle.

97) The SS (Schutzstaffel: a major paramilitary organization under Adolf Hitler and the Nazi Party in Nazi Germany) executed all of Hitler's political opponents and anyone within Germany who spoke out against Hitler's actions or objected to inhumane orders. They executed eighty four generals on suspicion that they were plotting against Hitler. Even though Hitler was democratically

elected, he turned into a dictator, and he wouldn't allow any real political opposition in Germany during WWII.

98) The allied forces lost more than 20,000 aircrafts during WWII. The US Army Air Force (the predecessor to the US Air Force) lost 9,949 aircrafts, while the Royal Air Force lost 11,965 aircrafts.

99) After attempting and failing to develop nuclear weapons, the Nazis built a dirty bomb which they intended to transport across the Pacific on a submarine, and to detonate it on the American West Coast. The uranium for the dirty bomb was lost on its way to Japan, and many have speculated that it was seized by the Americans and used to make the bombs that were dropped on Hiroshima and Nagasaki.

100) Nazi scientists developed effective biological weapons during WWII, but Hitler wouldn't allow such weapons to be used in battle. Some historians believe that he personally had bad experiences with such weapons as a soldier in WWI, so he didn't want them out there. Biological weapons were just as likely to kill the German soldiers using them, as they were to kill enemy soldiers.

101) Queen Elizabeth served as a mechanic and a driver during WWII. Even though she was just a teenager, she served in the Auxiliary Territorial Service, repairing engines for a fleet of military vehicles.

Princess Elizabeth Undergoing Instruction at the Auxiliary Territorial Service Training Centre (Front row, sitting between the two dogs)

102) An American Soldier named John McKinney single-handedly fought off a hundred Japanese soldiers. McKinney was standing guard at a military establishment in the Philippines when Japanese soldiers stormed the place. He fought off and killed a total of thirty eight attackers, first with gunfire, then with his bare hands. He was awarded the Medal of Honor.

103) Japanese scientists tried to develop a death ray that could kill people from several miles away. However, their first model was a failure. It could only kill its target from half a mile (800 meters) away, provided that the target didn't move for ten whole minutes. The Japanese eventually decided to abandon that project.

104) Adolf Hitler had a private train that was codenamed "Amerika", an odd choice given the fact that the US was his adversary during WWII. The train served as his

mobile home and office whenever he would travel around Germany or visit occupied territories. The train's name was changed after America joined the war.

105) The Nazis came very close to acquiring large amounts of plutonium during WWII. When the Germans went into Norway, they took over a factory that produced heavy water (a liquid that is used in nuclear reactors) which they could use to produce plutonium. However, a special team of Norwegian soldiers destroyed the factory with explosives, so the Nazis weren't able to use it.

106) Throughout the war, Germany and Britain fought for control of the Atlantic Ocean in what was known as the Battle of the Atlantic. The Germans tried to sink all ships that supplied goods to Britain. On the other side, the Royal Navies of Britain and Canada, and later the US Navy, fought off the Germans in a bid to protect merchant shipping lines.

107) Germany considered using potato beetles to destroy Britain's potato crop. The plan would involve dropping forty million beetles from German aircraft onto British potato fields. The Nazis were able to breed several million beetles, but they didn't manage to get to the forty million before the war ended. The idea was that by destroying the British food supply, they would weaken the whole country, and lower morale for the war.

108) The Soviet army trained over 2,000 women as snipers. Some of these women became the deadliest sharpshooters to ever grace the battlefield. A few were

individually credited with killing hundreds of German soldiers.

Women in the Russian and Soviet military

109) The Buchenwald concentration camp was run by Master Sergeant Martin Sommer, a brutal Nazi who came to be known as "Hangman of Buchenwald." Sommer would hang people by the wrists and let them wail in agony until they died.

110) In the earlier stages of WWII, Hitler had hoped that after invading and capturing France, Britain would sign a peace agreement and let him have control over most of Europe. At the time, the US and USSR were still neutral. Britain wouldn't agree to any of Hitler's conditions, and together with its dominions, it stood up to the Nazis until the other allies joined the fight.

111) Japan attacked Pearl Harbor on a Sunday because they knew that it was a day of rest in most Western countries (which were primarily Christian). They figured that

Americans were more likely to be caught off-guard on a Sunday.

112) You've probably heard of Auschwitz before, but do you know just how many souls were taken in this camp? Auschwitz was the deadliest of all Nazi concentration camps during WWII. Over a million people had died in that camp by the end of the war. When the camp was fully operational, 6,000 people were killed there every single day. Of the 7,500 Nazis who worked at that camp, only 750 of them were punished after the war, and most of the others went free.

Auschwitz concentration camp

113) At the Dauchau Concentration Camp located in Southern Germany, Nazi officers would line up Soviet POWs and shoot them for target practice.

114) Operation Dynamo was one of the most daring large-scale operations of WWII. Over three hundred thousand British troops and 140,000 allied troops were

rescued from behind enemy lines at Dunkirk Beach in France after the area fell under German control.

115) D-Day (June 6, 1944) was (and still remains) the largest, sea, land and air military operation in history. It was the beginning of the allied invasion of Europe. Over one hundred thousand amphibious troops landed on the Beaches of Normandy, and 20,000 paratroopers jumped into France (which was under German occupation at the time). The invasion of Normandy was led by General Dwight D. Eisenhower, who went on to become the President of the United States. To date, he remains one of the most revered military men in US history.

116) After the fall of Berlin, twenty-four top Nazi leaders were tried for war crimes during what came to be known as the Nuremberg Trials. At least half of them were sentenced to death.

117) Italian leader Benito Mussolini was executed on April 28, 1945, when the axis powers were about to fall.

118) Some Nazi commanders secretly negotiated the terms of surrender with the allied forces even before Berlin was captured. However, these negotiations were kept secret until after Hitler was dead.

119) The Japanese surrendered not just because of the atomic bombing of Hiroshima and Nagasaki, but also because the Soviets were finally planning to invade their territory, and they didn't have the manpower or resources to fight them back.

120) France was freed from Nazi occupation on August 25, 1944, by allied troops. Encouraged by news of the allied invasion, French fighters started resisting German control from within, and many German soldiers had actually fled Paris by the time allied troops got there.

121) The invasion of Normandy was the key turning point that led to victory for the allied forces. Four hundred and twenty five thousand combatants died during the invasion, but in the end, it led to the liberation of France and Belgium by the end of 1944.

122) Adolf Hitler committed suicide on April 30, 1945, while hiding in his bunker in Berlin. The USSR Red Army was closing in, and he didn't want to be captured.

123) Before the United States dropped atomic bombs on Japan, it air-dropped thousands of notices over more than thirty five Japanese cities, warning that the cities would soon be destroyed and that civilians should move out.

124) When Nazi soldiers came for the Jewish population in the Polish town of Rozwadow, two doctors created a fake typhus epidemic. The Nazis, who were afraid of contracting the disease, decided to keep away from the town. Eight thousand Jews were saved because of this act of trickery.

125) Before deciding to kill all Jewish people, the Nazis had considered deporting all of them to the island of Madagascar in the Indian Ocean. The Germans thought that the Jews would die of starvation in Madagascar because of the harsh conditions there. However, this plan was never put to action because the Germans figured out

that it would just be easier to put the Jews in concentration camps.

126) Japan tried to start a bubonic plague outbreak in China by dropping fleas infected with the disease into a Chinese city. There were several outbreaks of the disease in the area, but the plague didn't happen on the scale that Japan had hoped for.

127) Some scholars have argued that WWII was a continuation of WWI with a long break in between. That's because most countries fought on the same side that they did in the previous war, and many of the conditions that led to WWII were a direct result of how WWI ended. The Germans annexed Austria and other countries because they needed more land, labor, and other resources to pay their WWI reparation debts faster and build wealth for themselves.

128) Hitler's political party was called the National Socialist Party. Initially, it was abbreviated as "Naso." It later came to be known as the Nazi Party after a journalist named Konrad Heiden used the Bavarian word "Nazi" which meant "simple-minded" to make fun of Hitler and his followers.

Nazi Party

129) Hollywood movies helped shape Americans' understanding of the Nazis and the Japanese during the war. The movie studios were sympathetic to the Allies from the very beginning of the war, so they replaced gangster villains with Nazis, and they portrayed Japanese soldiers as inhumane and psychopathic.

130) The US and New Zealand tried to develop "tsunami bombs" during WWII. These were devices that were meant to be detonated to create a thity-three-foot (ten meter) tsunami that would wash over entire cities that were located next to the beach. These weapons were tested in New Zealand, but they were never used in battle.

131) Hitler considered the fall of Paris and occupation of France as payback for France's victory during WWI. When France was about to surrender to the Nazi's during WWII, Hitler ordered the Nazis to tear down the Paris Museum where WWI memorabilia was displayed. On his orders, the railway cabins in which the Germans signed

the WWI armistice were returned to the exact location where the event took place, as a way of undoing Germany's past failure and humiliating the French.

132) The London Zoo killed all snakes and other venomous animals during WWII because they were concerned that the zoo would be destroyed during air raids, and the animals would escape and harm people.

133) Whenever the allied forces captured high-ranking German officers, they would send them to live in a luxurious guarded building in Trent Park. The Nazi officers were treated well, but this was a plan to make them relax and lower their guard. It turns out that the building was wired with microphones, and British Intelligence Services listened to their conversations and learned a lot about what was going on in Berlin. For example, Britain learned that many Nazi officers actually thought Hitler was mad.

134) A Muslim cleric named Si Kaddour Benghabrit saved the lives of hundreds of Jews by hiding them in the Paris Grand Mosque and providing them with fake papers to conceal their identities. Despite the widespread bitterness between Muslims and Jews at that time, the cleric was willing to set aside those differences to help save Jewish lives.

135) As the red army retreated during the German invasion of the Soviet Union, the soldiers would destroy most buildings that were suitable for use as command posts. They would then wire the few remaining suitable buildings with explosives and set them to detonate after a week

or so. This way, they managed to kill high ranking German military officials and cripple Nazi operations.

136) One Japanese soldier named Hiroo Onoda never heard the news that Japan had surrendered after WWII. His entire unit was killed in battle, so he hid in the forest on an island in the Philippines. He held his position and waited for thirty years. When he was found in the forest in 1974, he wouldn't believe that Japan had lost the war. He refused to go back home, thinking it was all a trick, and they had to bring in his old commander to convince him that the war was over.

137) Three-quarters of all those who served in submarines during WWII were killed in battle by the end of the war.

138) From the time America entered WWII to the time the war ended, the manufacture of civilian cars came to a standstill. While three million cars were made in 1941, only 139 cars were made between 1942 and the end of the war in mid-1945. All car makers were focused on manufacturing military vehicles.

139) A polish midwife named Stanislawa Leszczynska delivered over 3,000 newborn babies in Auschwitz. Only twenty five of those children survived by the time the concentration camp was liberated.

140) Henry Ford and Adolf Hitler mutually admired each other. They both had pictures of each other on their desks. Although Henry Ford still remains one of the greatest American industrialists of all time, his views on Hitler and white supremacy left a dark mark on his legacy.

141) Hitler told his generals to collect thousands of Jewish artefacts so that when Germany won the war and succeeded in killing all Jews, he would create a "Museum of an Extinct Race."

142) A Spanish double agent named Joan Pujol Garcia worked for Britain and Germany at the same time during WWII. He was given medals in both countries for his distinguished service.

143) Russia and Japan never signed a peace treaty after WWII. That means that the two countries never officially acknowledged that the war was over between them. At least on paper, the two countries are still technically at war even today.

144) After Hitler invaded the Soviet Union, he told the Nazis that he wanted them to kill everyone in Moscow and then turn the entire city into an artificial lake.

145) The allies created a plan to make Hitler less aggressive by adding oestrogen (the female sex hormone) to his food supply. They had first considered poisoning Hitler, but they decided against it because he had food tasters. Oestrogen, on the other hand, was a tasteless chemical, and its effects would be delayed, so no one would suspect anything was wrong. The plan was cancelled because British assets in Berlin were too afraid to carry it out.

146) German soldiers who fought in WWII were given large amounts of methamphetamine. At the time, it was believed that the drug could keep soldiers alert and increase their endurance on the battlefield.

147) After leading Britain into victory during WWII, Prime Minister Winston Churchill was voted out of office in the middle of ongoing peace conferences.

148) The British military used special searchlights called "Moonlight Batteries" to create artificial moonlight that was used to guide troop movements during the war.

149) A Flight Sergeant named Nicholas Alkemade fell 18,000 feet (5.5 kilometers) without a parachute when his aircraft was destroyed by enemy fire. He miraculously survived, and his only injury was a sprained leg.

150) When allied troops landed on Normandy Beach, they opened a second front in the land war against Germany. Up to that point, Germany had only been fighting on the Eastern front (against the Soviets), so for the first time, they had to divide their land troops into two, which weakened them significantly.

151) The BBC (British Broadcasting Corporation) was involved in the planning stages before D-Day. The British military used the media organization to run a contest where people would send in holiday photos taken at French beaches and the person with the best photo would win. The photos were collected and analysed, so that the allies could figure out which areas were suitable for an amphibious landing. Over 7,000 ships were used in the landing of Normandy. British Prime Minister Winston Churchill wanted to go to sea and watch the landing first hand, but several generals advised him against it. He only backed down when King George VI said that if Churchill went to the battlefront, he too would come along.

Operation Overlord

152) The allies used deception campaigns (mostly spreading false rumors) to keep the Germans guessing on where exactly they planned to land when they invaded France. As a result, Germany had to split its troops to cover different beaches, which made them vulnerable.

153) The phrase "loose lips sink ships" was coined during WWII. There was concern that German spies were all over Britain, and if anyone talked carelessly about the war, they could accidentally leak information to the spies and it could result in the loss of life.

154) The phrase "loose lips sink ships" was coined during WWII. There was concern that German spies were all over Britain, and if anyone talked carelessly about the war, they could accidentally leak information to the spies and it could result in the loss of life.

155) After America joined WWII, General George Patton was considered the best general that the allied forces had.

The Germans were aware of this fact. In the lead up to D-Day, the allies used General Patton to trick the Germans into thinking they intended to land at Kent instead of Normandy. They built some dummy equipment near Kent, and they made sure that General Patton was spotted by German informants on his way to Kent. The trick worked so well, that even after the landing of Normandy, the Germans still kept some of their best troops at Kent, expecting a second landing.

156) D-day was an international effort with fighters from many different countries, so the allied forces had to overcome lots of cultural differences, language barriers, and issues that arose from unclear chains of command, to make the invasion work. Most fighters were American, British and Canadian, but there were also fighters from Australia, Belgium, France, Greece, Norway, Rhodesia, Poland, Holland, and Czech.

157) British scientists designed a "life pod" to protect Prime Minister Winston Churchill during high altitude flights. Churchill's doctors were concerned that a man of his age could die during such flights because airplane cabins weren't properly pressurized back then. The life pod was too big to fit in the plane, so Churchill never actually used it.

158) The Germans developed the 88mm anti-tank and anti-aircraft artillery gun. It was widely used in the Soviet and North African theaters of war, and it was one of the most feared weapons of the entire war. The artillery gun could fire 17-pound (7kg) grenades, which could go up to several thousand feet into the air, burst into over 1,500

metallic shards, and destroy anything flying within 200 yards (182 meters) of the explosion.

159) Some members of the British Royal Family, along with some influential aristocrats, had links to the Nazis before WWII started. For example, Edward VIII, who had been king just before the war, admired Hitler greatly.

160) Japan attacked Pearl Harbor (in Hawaii) because America had imposed crippling sanctions on them. The sanctions were a result of the atrocities they had committed in China, and many other pacific territories, some of which were under American control at the time.

161) The term "axis powers" was coined when Benito Mussolini gave a speech right after Germany and Italy signed a treaty. In that speech, he stated that Europe and the whole world would revolve around "the axis of Rome and Berlin," meaning that those two cities would run the whole world.

162) When the Germans invaded the Soviet Union, they opened the largest land theater of war in the history of the world. The German invasion was known as Operation Barbarossa. The operation finally failed partly because German fighters weren't used to harsh Russian winters.

163) Pearl Harbor is located more than 2,000 miles (3200 kilometers) away from Japan. Because of this distance, no one expected such a daring attack, and the harbor was left unguarded most of the time. The US Navy didn't have anti aircraft guns ready for such an event and wasn't able to retaliate.

164) Polish soldiers in Italy used a bear called Wojtek to transport ammunition. The bear was domesticated and trained to work in a circus, and got along with the soldiers quite well.

Wojtek the bear

165) When the allied air forces raided Germany during the night, all cities turned off their lights so that they would be less visible to the pilots. The German city of Constance, which is located near Germany's border with Switzerland, was the only one that left its lights shining bright. Allied pilots didn't bomb the city of Constance because it was unclear where Switzerland ended and where Constance began. The allies didn't want to accidentally drop bombs on a neutral country.

166) It's believed that Hitler was taking a nap when news got to Berlin that the Allied forces had landed on Normandy. All of his men were apparently afraid to wake him up and give him the bad news because he often had angry outbursts when things weren't going his way.

167) Apart from London, other British cities that were targeted by German air raids included Swansea, Liverpool, Birmingham, and Bristol.

168) During WWII, America banned radio stations from receiving song requests from listeners. They feared that German spies could use song requests to send coded messages back and forth.

169) The Soviet Union was one of the first countries to have women fight on the frontlines in combat. This had to do with them embracing communism, which encouraged equality in the workplace as well as in the military. More than a million women served in the Red Army during WWII.

170) Many fascists fled Europe after WWII. They escaped through networks of secret organizations known as "ratlines", and they settled in South America, Australia, the Middle East, and Canada.

171) Finland switched sides during the war. When WWII started, Finland was already at war with the Soviet Union, so they sought the help of the Germans to fight off the Soviets. However, after signing a peace treaty with the Soviets, Finland re-evaluated its position, and it switched sides to fight against the Germans.

172) Only 11% of the 2,800 Japanese Kamikaze pilots hit their targets in Pearl Harbor. The other 89% either didn't make it all the way, or they missed the targets they were aiming for, and instead hit the water.

173) Claus Von Stauffenberg, a German General who disliked Hitler's inhumane policies, tried to kill him using a suitcase bomb. Hitler survived with a scratch, and General Stauffenberg was executed.

174) During the war, America created special decks of playing cards that their servicemen carried into battle. When soldiers were captured (or trapped behind enemy lines), they could pour water over the cards, thus revealing maps and escape routes printed with invisible ink.

175) Fanta, the world-famous soft drink, was developed in Germany during WWII. The country couldn't get the ingredients required to manufacture Coca-Cola during the war (because of trade restrictions), so the soda company decided to make a similar soft drink with locally available ingredients; and that's how they came up with Fanta.

176) Apart from Jewish people, Romanise, ethnic Slavs, gay people, Jehovah's Witnesses, and people with communist leanings were also murdered or persecuted in Germany and Nazi-occupied territories.

177) Spain, Sweden, Switzerland, and Ireland were among the few countries that remained neutral throughout the duration of WWII.

178) Penicillin was a very valuable antibiotic during WWII, but its supply was scarce. To deal with the shortages, the army collected soldiers' urine and processed it to recycle penicillin.

179) A woman named Irena Sendler rescued over 2,500 Jewish children from the ghettos of Warsaw during WWII.

She would take the children, give them new identities, and set them up with other families. She buried a jar containing proof of the real identities of the children in her backyard, hoping to reunite them with their parents after the war. However, most of the parents were killed in camps before the war ended, and the reunions never happened. Still, thousands of children were alive because of her brave actions.

180) Anne Frank is one of the most iconic figures of WWII. She was born in Frankfurt Germany to a Jewish family, but they fled the country shortly afterward because of rising anti-Semitic attitudes. Her family settled in Amsterdam and they were doing well until the Nazis invaded the Netherlands. Her family had to go into hiding for two years during the war. Throughout this period, Anne kept a diary, which has been very important for historians seeking to understand what it was like to be Jewish in Europe during WWII. Anne's family was captured by the Nazis, and she and her sister were sent to Bergen-Belsen Camp, where she died in 1945.

Anne Frank

181) 80% of all deaths in WWII occurred in just four countries: Russia, China, Germany, and Poland.

182) The allies (China, USA, Britain, the Soviet Union, and France) became the permanent members of the United Nations Security Council.

183) USA and Canada loaned a lot of money, supplies, and weaponry to Britain and the Soviet Union during WWII. After the war, the Soviet Union refused to pay its debt, while Britain slowly paid it off for the next fifty one years.

184) The Nazis had at least sixty eight camps where they detained civilians and POWs across Europe during WWII. They included main camps (mostly collection camps), labor camps, concentration camps, and extermination camps.

185) Some American soldiers started collecting the skulls of the Japanese soldiers they had killed. They took skulls and other body parts as trophies, and some would send dried bones back home to their friends and families. The military leadership discouraged this practice, but it didn't do enough to stop it.

186) Between twelve and fourteen million ethnic Germans who were born in other countries around Europe were deported back to Germany after WWII ended. Many of them had never been to Germany before.

187) America and Britain used German POWs for slave labor. Forcing POWs to work as slaves was against the

Geneva Convention, so to get around this, the POWs were paid extremely low wages.

188) The Germans and the Soviets both had "scorched earth" policies during WWII. Under these policies, when a territory was about to fall into the hands of opposing forces, the retreating army would burn buildings and farms, and destroy railways or any other infrastructure that the enemy might use.

Ruined Kiev (Ukraine)

189) America turned away possibly hundreds of thousands of Jewish refugees throughout WWII. Similarly, Britain had in place immigration laws that were hard to navigate, so Jewish refugees had a difficult time getting into the country. The allies however, weren't totally aware of the horror that was going on in Nazi camps until the later years of the war.

190) After WWII, Germany lost a quarter of the territory it had before the war started. Its territories were taken by Poland and the Soviet Union. The allies split Germany into two states. East Germany, was put under

the control of the Soviet Union, and West Germany was taken over by the Western Allies. Austria was also sanctioned by the allies after WWII. It was occupied by the victorious allies until 1955 when it became an independent state.

191) Germany's currency during WWII was known as the Reichsmark. It was originally introduced in 1924. When the Nazis took over, they changed its design to include the swastika and other Nazi symbols. The currency was discontinued in 1948, three years after the war.

20 Reichsmark paper

192) Although the bombing of civilian cities is considered a war crime today, there was no specific international humanitarian or customary law that prohibited the practice during WWII. The US bombed sixty seven civilian cities in Japan during the war and Germany, Britain, and most other powers did the same thing at different stages during the war.

193) The Universal Declaration of Human rights came in 1948, three years after the end of WWII, but it was a direct result of the war. It laid the groundwork for the end

of colonialism around the world, and the civil rights movements that started within a decade after the war.

194) The atomic bombs dropped on Hiroshima and Nagasaki were developed under the Manhattan Project, a nuclear research and development project headed by Robert Oppenheimer. The project had several physics labs located in Manhattan, but the actual bombs were built in New Mexico, far away from any population centers. Americans dropped the first nuclear bomb in Hiroshima on August 6, 1945, and the second one in Nagasaki three days later.

195) Both the German and the Japanese military tested newly developed weapons on civilians before allowing them to be mass-produced and used on the battlefield.

196) When Japan invaded countries in East Asia, it termed them "The Greater East Asia Co-Prosperity Sphere." Japan wanted people in its Asian territories to think of it as a liberator that was freeing them from European colonialists. This worked in some places. However, public opinion quickly turned against Japan after many in Asia learned about their brutal war tactics.

197) Germany economically exploited the countries it occupied during WWII. By the end of the war, the Nazis had collected 69.5 billion Reichsmarks (about $27.8 billion) from other European countries, including France, Denmark, Norway, Czechoslovakia, and other territories.

198) WWII led to the development of artificial harbors. Fleets had to be docked at strategic places, not just areas

with natural harbors. Most of the early artificial harbors were set up along the English Channel.

199) The world's first programmable computers were designed for use during WWII. These included the Z3 computer, the ENIAC computer, and the Colossus.

200) Two-thirds of all munitions used by the allied forces in WWII were produced by the Americans. That included warplanes, warships, tanks, artillery, and land transportation equipment such as lorries.

201) Armies on both sides of the conflict had more mobility during WWII than they did during WWI. WWII tanks were faster, and they were the primary weapons on the battlefield, not just the support weapons. As WWII went on, new batches of tanks became better armoured, and their firepower improved significantly.

American M36 tank destroyers during Battle of the Bulge

202) The Soviets put captured Nazi soldiers in "Gulag" labor camps. The conditions in these camps were terrible. Prisoners were overworked, underfed, and there were numerous deaths.

203) Portable machine guns became popular during WWII. Before that, machine guns were bulky and each one had to be operated by a small team. However, during WWII the machine gun was redesigned to be compact enough so that it could be carried around and used by just one person.

204) The Allies were able to out-produce the Axis powers (when it came to manufacturing weapons and supplying food to their soldiers), not just because they had stronger economies back home, but also because they allowed women to join the workforce. In Nazi Germany, women weren't expected to work in industries, because they were encouraged to stay home and become "good mothers."

205) Instead of using codebooks as they had done in previous wars, various armies decided to design ciphering machines. The German "Enigma Machine" is the most well-known of these devices.

206) During WWII, unlike previous wars, airplanes could be used to airlift high-priority supplies, equipment, and even to transport servicemen. This was a great advancement because it allowed armies on both sides to get to the battlefront in the shortest time possible. This made it possible for armies to move very rapidly and conquer large territories in a matter of days.

207) After losing many ships to German submarines during WWI, Britain put a lot of resources into developing submarine defence technologies, which came in handy during WWII. They developed sonar (which was useful in detecting the positions of German submarines), and they perfected the use of convoys to protect their ships.

208) The death rate in Japanese labour camps was at 27.1%, which was seven times higher than the death rate in Italian and German labor camps. The death rate was especially high for American POWs; 37% of all Americans captured by the Japanese died in labour camps.

209) As a result of the raid on Pearl Harbor (and similar raids in Taranto and the Coral Sea), it became clear that aircraft carriers were better investments than battleships because carriers were equipped to defend themselves against air attacks. America and its allies started developing carriers in place of battleships.

210) 80% of all males born in the Soviet Union in the year 1923 died during WWII. Most of these men were only sixteen or seventeen years old when the war started in 1939.

211) More Soviet soldiers and civilians died in the Battle of Stalingrad alone (the deadliest battle of the entire war) than American and British soldiers combined over the course of the entire war.

212) The US Air Corps lost more servicemen than the US Marine Corps during WWII. Those who served in the Air Corps had a 71% chance of dying. Many were shot down,

including George H.W. Bush, who was rescued by the Navy and went on to become the 41st US President decades later.

213) German forces never attacked the US mainland, although they had bombers that were within the range of the US East Coast, particularly New York City. At first, Germany had hoped that America would stay out of the war. When America joined the war, they were mainly focused on fighting the Japanese at first, and the Germans tried to avoid putting themselves in America's crosshairs.

214) A Japanese fighter pilot named Hiroyoshi Nishizawa is credited with shooting down more than eighty American and Allied airplanes during WWII.

Hiroyoshi Nishizawa

215) In the lead up to the war, Hitler and the Nazis used posters, cartoons, and films to play on anti-Semitic senti-

ments in Germany, as groundwork for the holocaust that followed. One Nazi newspaper falsely claimed that Jews kidnapped and killed little German children because they needed the blood of Christian children for use during Jewish religious rituals.

216) Afghanistan remained neutral throughout the war, but it had close relationships with the three main Axis powers. In 1940, Afghanistan was banking on Germany winning the war; it made an official request to Germany to give it control over some more land in British India in the event that Germany won.

217) Due to international pressure to condemn the actions of the Nazis, some countries which had remained neutral throughout most of WWII (including Argentina and much of South America) were forced to declare war on Germany just months before the whole war came to an end.

218) After the fall of France, its colonies in Africa (e.g. Algeria and Morocco) fell under the control of Nazi Germany. Vichy France (an unoccupied state in France that answered to Germany) oversaw most activities in these colonies until the allies retook the states after winning what came to be known as The Campaign for North Africa.

219) Australia declared war on Germany on the 3rd of September, 1939, because at the time, it was legally bound to be at war with any country upon which Britain declared war.

220) After Germany invaded Belgium, its colonies in Africa, especially Belgian-Congo, remained within the control of the allies. Congo was very valuable because it was rich in natural resources that were crucial for the war. The uranium used to make the nuclear bombs that were dropped in Japan was mostly sourced from mines in the Congo.

221) There were no battles in Antarctica during WWII, but it was the subject of serious competition between the Axis powers and the Allied powers. Even before the war broke out, Nazi Germany sent explorers to the continent, and it laid claim to large areas of the continent. During the war, the United States and Britain both set up bases in Antarctica so that they would have a permanent presence there and keep Germany from claiming any more of the frozen continent.

222) In the lead up to WWII, Belgium declared that they would be neutral in the event that another war broke out in Europe. However, that only made them an easy mark for the Germans who invaded Belgium on their way to France.

223) Before the war, most islands in the Caribbean were under British control. However, since Britain needed weaponry it couldn't pay for, it made an agreement with the US. America would take British military bases in the Caribbean in exchange for several destroyers and other supplies. Even before America joined the war, it protected the Caribbean Islands and shipped tons of supplies from the Gulf of Mexico, through the Islands, and to North Africa and Europe.

224) At the beginning of WWII, China's army had 2.6 million soldiers. By the end of the war, the army had increased its numbers to 5.7 million soldiers. Throughout the war, the Chinese Army suffered a total of 3.2 million casualties.

Chinese soldiers poorly armed, snuggled close to the land for camouflage

225) Some European countries were totally defenceless when WWII broke out. Denmark, for example, tried to resist the German invasion on April 9, 1940, but were overwhelmed within just a few hours, and they let the Germans take over the country.

226) The city of Brazzaville in the Republic of Congo technically served as the capital of France between 1940 and 1943 during WWII. When Paris fell, the government of France went into exile, and it formed "Free France" outside the borders of the country. Free France, with the help of the allies, retained control of French colonies in

Africa, and Brazzaville was chosen as the capital for the government in exile.

227) Indonesia gained independence as a result of WWII. Before the war, it was a colony of the Netherlands and it was called Dutch East Indies. During the war, in 1941, Japan outfought the Dutch and allied troops and took control of Indonesia. Even as battles raged on in the Pacific, Indonesia remained under the control of Japan, until Japan surrendered at the end of the war. Five days after Japan surrendered, Indonesia declared its independence. The declaration was followed by the Indonesian National Revolution, and three years later, the country was totally free.

228) Emperor Haile Selassie of Ethiopia was kicked out of his country in 1936 by the Italians who wanted to colonize the country. He sought refuge in Britain, and he had been trying to get the allies to support him against the Italians. Luckily for him, when WWII broke out, his interests and those of the British Empire were aligned. Britain brought in troops from its African colonies, including Ghana, Kenya, Nigeria, and several other territories. The allies were able to retake Addis Ababa (the Ethiopian capital) in what came to be known as the East African Campaign.

229) Mahatma Gandhi was arrested by the British Government in India for leading a movement that called for India's independence during WWII. Britain heavily relied on the support of the Indian Empire (which included India, Pakistan, and Bangladesh), so they did everything they could to destroy Nationalist movements that were cropping up in the territory.

230) At the beginning of WWII, Iran was neutral, but Britain was worried that German nationals living in Iran had Nazi influence and they could potentially take control of Iran's oil fields. Britain, therefore, invaded Iran with the help of the soviets, kicked out the Shah (leader) and replaced him with his son who was friendlier to the allies. As a result, Iran joined WWII on the side of the allies.

231) When Britain was recruiting fighters from Mandatory Palestine (what's now Israel and Palestine) for WWII, it made sure that it enlisted an equal number of Jewish and Arab soldiers. That way, after the war, no side would have a stronger army than the other, and peace could be maintained in the region.

232) Ireland was the only member of the British Commonwealth to remain neutral throughout WWII. Britain briefly considered invading Ireland to take over some of its ports for use during the war, but they decided against it. Germany did bomb the Irish City of Dublin because some private Irish citizens were aiding the allies.

233) Two and a half million Indian soldiers fought in WWII under British Command. India had the largest army raised through voluntary enlistment (other armies drafted most of their fighters).

Indian troops in Burma

234) Although Iran and the Soviet Union fought on the same side during WWII, the Soviets saw the war as an opportunity to take over control of some Iranian territories. They stirred up issues between the Iranian government and the Azerbaijani and Kurdish people, leading to both groups leaving Iran immediately after the war.

235) Iraq was the stage for a proxy war (smaller conflict) between Britain and Germany during WWII. Iraqi Prime Minister Nuri al-Said cooperated with the British, and as a result, he was overthrown by Rashid Ali who was backed by Germany. Britain then invaded Iraq and made the country declare war on Germany, but the Germans didn't recognize the war declaration because they didn't consider the British-controlled Iraqi government to be legitimate.

236) After the war, Switzerland was accused of helping the Nazis by allowing them to keep proceeds from the Holocaust in their banks.

237) Although Spain was neutral during the war, it mobilized a massive army to defend itself against invasion from both the allies and the Axis powers. As a result, both sides did their best to stay out of Spain because they didn't want another powerful enemy.

238) Japan occupied Korea during WWII, and after it surrendered, the Korean Peninsula was split into two. The north was occupied by the Soviets and the south by America. The conflict of ideas between the two superpowers led to the Korean War and the formation of North and South Korea.

239) The Jewish Community in Palestine was at odds with Britain during WWII because Britain had restricted Jewish immigration to Palestine. However, the community saw Britain as their best ally when it came to saving fellow Jews in Nazi-controlled Europe, so they set their differences aside and joined forces during WWII.

240) General Douglas MacArthur commanded American troops in the Philippines during WWII. When Japan invaded the Philippines, he was ordered to move to Australia with other high ranking officials and leave his troops behind. He swore that he would return to the Philippines at any cost. He defended Australia for a while, as he rallied support for his plan to retake the Philippines. Two years after leaving the Philippines, he kept his promise and returned with more troops, and fought for the next ten months to free the country. Today, General MacArthur is considered one of the greatest and most inspirational military leaders in the history of America.

241) Hitler had a plan in place to invade Switzerland in 1940, but he decided that it would be a waste of resources. Switzerland had a fairly strong army and its mountainous landscape gave it a great advantage. Switzerland declared that it was on its own side during the war, and it actually shot down a few German aircraft for violating its airspace.

242) After Japan raided Pearl Harbor, between 110,000 and 120,000 Japanese-Americans were moved from their homes and into internment camps (forced relocation and incarceration in concentration camps). This was a violation of their basic rights, but America thought that it was necessary to root out Axis spies. Today, this is still one of the most shameful acts performed by the US Government in modern times.

Pearl Harbor Attack

243) The Vatican was mostly silent during WWII. Vatican City (and the Holy See) had a treaty with Italy that required them to stay politically neutral, so they were

bound to stay out of Mussolini's war business. Still, Pope Pius XII occasionally spoke out against racism throughout the war.

244) In the lead up to WWII, the Nazis introduced Nuremberg Laws which classified people into Aryans and Non-Aryans. The Aryans were considered a superior race, and the mixing of races was prohibited under the law. The Nazis also resolved to teach Germans to think of non-Aryans as sub-human.

245) The US Military was ready to put women in combat roles during WWII, but public opinion was generally against women serving in such positions. Women, therefore, only served in uniformed auxiliary roles. 350,000 American women volunteered for auxiliary service. They worked mostly as nurses, administrators, mechanics, drivers, and electricians. In the UK, women were drafted by the Department of Labour to join auxiliary services. Women in Canada formed the Women's Volunteer Service. Many women signed up from all over Canada. The service grew so large, and it was so well organized, that the Canadian government eventually decided to create the Canadian Women's Army Corps.

246) Britain was able to get more women into the workforce during WWII by promoting the idea of the "home front." The government made it clear that the home front was just as important as the battlefront, and if the home front was weak, Britain would lose at the battlefront.

247) During WWII, the US Government created over 200,000 different posters aimed at different groups in the

country. The Office of War Information created posters targeting men, women, and people of color to join the war. They also created posters targeted at affluent people, asking them to buy war bonds.

248) In Nazi propaganda, Americans were represented as gangsters and cowardly murderers, just like Al Capone (who was world-famous at the time).

249) The US Government used radio programs to spread pro-war propaganda during WWII. President Roosevelt himself had "fireside chats" where he encouraged America to support the troops.

250) The US Government encouraged the creation of "Victory Gardens" during WWII. People were urged to plant vegetable gardens in their backyards to help prevent food shortages. Through the media, the government asked women and children to plant these gardens as a patriotic duty, hence the name "Victory Gardens."

Plant a Vitory Garden poster

ALSO BY SCOTT MATTHEWS

Check out our most popular title: '3666 Interesting, Fun And Crazy Facts You Won't Believe Are True'. Search for it on Amazon to get your copy today!

Did you enjoy the book or learn something new? It really helps out small publishers like French Hacking if you could leave a quick review on Amazon so others in the community can also find the book!

★★★★★

BONUS: 3666 INTERESTING, FUN AND CRAZY FACTS YOU WON'T BELIEVE ARE TRUE

1) It is false that you can bite through a finger as easily as a carrot. It takes 200 newtons to bite through a raw carrot and 1485 newtons just to cause a fracture to a finger.

2) It took over 22 centuries to complete the Great Wall of China. It was built, rebuilt and extended by many imperial dynasties and kingdoms. The wall exceeds 12,000 miles (20,000km).

3) The largest empire the world has ever seen was the British Empire which covered almost a quarter of the planet in its peak in 1920.

4) Most of the camels in Saudi Arabia are imported from Australia.

5) China produces the most pollution in the world contributing 30% of all the countries total. These come from coal, oil and natural gases.

6) There are currently 1.6 billion live websites on the web right now. However 99% of these sites you cannot access

through Google and is known as the Deep Web.

7) Just like all languages, sign language has different accents based on country, age, ethnicity and whether the person is deaf or not.

8) There are over 1200 different species of bats in the world and contrary to popular belief none of them are blind. Bats can hunt in the dark using echolocation, which means they use echoes of self-produced sounds bouncing off objects to help them navigate.

9) When you're buried six feet down in soil and without a coffin, an average adult body normally takes eight to twelve years to decompose to a skeleton.

10) Pigs are physically incapable to look up into the sky.

11) The largest detonated bomb in the world was the Tsar Bomba on October 30 in 1961 by the Soviet Union. The blast was 3,000 times stronger than the bomb used on Hiroshima. The impact was enough to break windows 560 miles (900km) away.

12) The wars between Romans and Persians lasted about 721 years, the longest conflict in human history.

13) There were at least forty two known assassination plots against Hitler.

14) It took approximately 75 years for the telephone to reach 50 million users, the radio 38 years, 13 years for the television, 4 for the Internet, 2 for Facebook and only 19 days for Pokemon Go.

15) The biggest island is the world is Greenland as Australia is a continent.

16) In 2018, 4 billion people have access to the internet yet 844 million people still don't have access to clean water.

17) A single teaspoon of water has eight times more atoms than there are teaspoons full of water in the Atlantic Ocean.

18) Ancient Egyptians used headrests made of stone instead of pillows.

19) France was the first country to introduce the registration plate on August 14th 1893.

20) The Netherlands was the first country to legalise same sex marriage which was in 2001.

21) The average human attention span has almost halved since 2000 decreasing from 20 seconds to 12 in 2018.

22) The oldest recorded tree in the world is reported to be 9,550 years old located in Dalarna, Sweden.

23) The oldest living system ever recorded is the Cyanobacterias, a type of bacteria that originated 2.8 billion years ago.

24) Being hungry causes serotonin levels to drop, causing a whirlwind of uncontrollable emotions including anxiety, stress and anger.

25) On Monday March 23, 2178, Pluto will complete its full orbit since its original discovery in 1930.

BONUS

Thanks for supporting me and purchasing this book! I'd like to send you some freebies. They include:

- The digital version of ***500 World War I & II Facts***

- The digital version of ***101 Idioms and Phrases***

- The audiobook for my best seller ***1144 Random Facts***

Scan the QR code below, enter your email, and I'll send you all the files. Happy reading!

www.ingramcontent.com/pod-product-compliance
Lightning Source LLC
Chambersburg PA
CBHW071352080526
44587CB00017B/3073